Cognitive Behavioral Therapy

The Complete Guide to Beat Anxiety, Depression, Anger, Panic Attacks and Negative Thoughts. Learn How to Improve your Mental Health and Regain Control of your Life

Table of Contents

Introduction 1

The History of Cognitive Behavioral Therapy 3

What Does CBT Treatment Resemble? 5

Doing Homework 6

The significance of the structure 6

Group sessions 7

How else does it vary from different therapies? 7

Who Benefits from Trying CBT? 8

Chapter 1 - Cognitive distortions 11

Essential CBT Techniques and Tools 18

CBT Interventions and Exercises 22

5 Final Cognitive Behavioral Activities 27

1. Mindfulness Meditation 27

2. Progressive Approximation 28

3. Keeping in touch with Self-Statements to Counteract Negative Thoughts 28

4. Imagine the Best Parts of Your Day 29

5. Reframe Your Negative Thoughts 30

6. A Take-Home Message 30

Chapter 2 - Raise your self-esteem 32

How is it to have low self-esteem? 32

Daniel's belief that he was useless and different 32

Parts of treatment that Daniel discovered accommodating

.... 33

What is low self-esteem? 34

What causes low self-esteem? 35

Build self-esteem 36

8 Steps to Improving Your Self-Esteem 38

1. Be careful. 39

2. Change the story. 39

3. Abstain from falling into the look at the and-despair rabbit hole. 40

4. Channel your inner rock star. 41

5. Exercise. 42

6. Do unto others. 42

7. Forgiveness 43

8. Recollect that you are not your circumstances 44

Chapter 3 - Transform your mentality **45**

The Three Rules of Neural Networks 47

What These Rules Mean for Therapy 49

Stop Negative Thoughts: Choosing a Healthier Way of Thinking 50

What is healthy thinking? 50

How does CBT assist you in intuition in a healthy way? 51

How can you stop your thoughts? 53

Different approaches to stop thought 56

An example of thought-stopping 57

Chapter 4 - What is Positive CBT? A Look at Positive Cognitive Behavioral Therapy **58**

What is Positive Cognitive Behavioral Therapy? 59

Positive CBT and Its Relationship with Other Theories and Therapies 60

Cognitive Behavioral Therapy (CBT).............................60

CBT Model 60

Cognitive Therapy (CT) 61

Rational Emotive Behavior Therapy (REBT)....................62

Solution Focused Brief Therapy (SFBT) 65

Functional Behavior Analysis (FBA) 66

Positive CBT vs. CBT: What's the Difference? 68

Fredrik Bannick on Practicing Positive CBT...................70

Positive CBT Interventions and Techniques....................72

Change the Viewing 73

Change the Doing 75

Change the Feeling 77

Homework..78

5 Positive CBT Exercises 79

1. Daily Exceptions Journal..80

2. Strengths Spotting by Exception Finding...................81

3. Three Good Things 82

4. Benefit Finding 82

5. You, At Your Best..83

A Take-Home Message 84

Chapter 5 - Cognitive-Behavioral Therapy for Depression and Anxiety 86

Cognitive Behavioral Therapy 86

Different Types of Cognitive-Behavioral Therapy.............. 87

Does CBT Work for Depression? 88

Medications or Psychotherapy?...................................... 89

Therapy for Anxiety Disorders 89

Cognitive-behavioral therapy (CBT) for anxiety 91

Thought to challenge in CBT for anxiety........................... 92

Exposure therapy for anxiety.. 93

Systematic desensitization 94

Complementary therapies for anxiety disorder 96

Making anxiety therapy work for you 98

Chapter 6 - How CBT to help in boosting mindfulness, resilience, assertiveness, and self-esteem 100

What is Mindfulness Therapy? (Definition) 100

Research and Studies on its Effectiveness 103

6 Mindfulness Therapy Techniques............................... 106

Different Types of Therapy That Incorporate Mindfulness 109

A Look at using it in a Group Context.............................111

Mindfulness Therapy for Couples...................................111

Care Therapy and Depression 112

Utilizing Mindfulness Therapy to Treat Anxiety............... 114

Will Mindfulness-Based Therapy Help Treat Insomnia?.. 116

3 Mindfulness Therapy Exercises and Games 116

1. Givens 117

2. Getting it done with Gratitude 117

3. Utilizing a Strengths Approach to Build Perspective-Taking Capacity 118

Care Therapy Training and Certification 119

A Take-Home Message.. 120

Chapter 7 - Getting Resilient Through Cognitive Behavioral Therapy **122**

The Three Cs of Resiliency 124

Assertiveness: What Is Assertiveness? 125

What Is Assertiveness Training? 126

Explanations behind Assertiveness Training.................... 126

What Is the Difference Between Assertiveness and Aggression? 127

What Is Cognitive Behavior Therapy? 128

Manifestation Effectiveness 132

Time for Mastery.. 132

Extraordinary Considerations 133

Step A: Determine Readiness for Assertiveness Training . 134

Step B. Language and Concepts Conversation Assertive Communication.. 137

Aggressive Communication 139

Latent Communication 140

Step C. Figure out how to Distinguish Between the Three Modes of Communication 140

Step D. Characterize Criteria for Measuring Change in Assertive Behavior 142

Step E. Identifying Mistaken Traditional Assumptions and Countering Them with Assertive Rights 142

Step F. Going up against Fears about Being Assertive 143

CBT#23-0005 SAMPLE Confronting Fears 143

Step G. Analysis as a Form of Manipulation 145

1. Acknowledgment... 148

2. Examining 149

3. Clouding 150

a. Agree in Part 151

b. Agree in Probability 152

c. Concur in Principle 152

4. Content-to-Process Shift 153

5. Break 154

6. Easing back down..155

7. Broken Record Procedure 156

Chapter 8 - Self-Esteem 159

What are simply the basic highlights of Low Esteem? 159

Can CBT Therapy be utilized for Low Self Esteem? 160

How is it to have low self-esteem? 162

Daniel's belief that he was useless and extraordinary .162

Parts of treatment that Daniel found helpful 163

What Causes Low Self-esteem? 163

What props is low self-esteem going?.....................165

Treatments for low self-esteem 166

Psychological treatments for low self-esteem 166

Medical treatments for low self-esteem 166

How might I overcome my low self-esteem? 166

Testing your anxious prediction 167

Distinguishing and challenging your self-criticism..........168

Retraining yourself to concentrate on the positive 169

Testing your bottom line and building another one..........170

Changing your rules and presumptions...................... 171

Practicing positive parts of your self-image with the goal that they win the memory retrieval competition....................172

Chapter 9 - Sleep disorders.................................... 174

How does cognitive behavioral therapy for sleeping disorders work? 174

Cognitive-behavioral therapy vs. pills 177

Insomnia and other disorders 177

Finding help 178

Who can benefit from cognitive behavioral therapy for sleep deprivation? 179

Therapy for Sleep Disorders............................. 180

What characterizes a sleep disorder? 181

Cognitive-behavioral therapy (CBT) for sleep disorders...181

How accomplishes CBT work for sleep disorders? 182

Utilizing a sleep diary in CBT 183

Thought to challenge in CBT 183

Testing negative thoughts that fuel sleep issues 184

Behavioral techniques utilized in CBT for sleep disorders186

Relaxation techniques for insomnia 188

Making therapy work for you 189

Chapter 10 - Cognitive Behavioral Therapy for Addiction 191

Cognitive Behavioral Therapy for Addiction..................192

What Is Cognitive Behavioral Therapy? 195

Role of Cognitive Behavioral Therapy in Addiction Treatment 196

Which Types Of Drug Addiction Does Cognitive Behavioral Therapy Treat? 197

Benefits of Cognitive Behavioral Therapy...................... 198

Length of Cognitive Behavioral Therapy Treatment.........199

What's to expect At Cognitive Behavioral Therapy Sessions? 200

Cognitive Behavioral Therapy in Use with Other Therapies 203

Role of Cognitive Behavioral Therapy in Dual Diagnosis Treatment...204

Chapter 11 - Achieve work-life balance 207

How to Have a Healthy Work/Life Balance...................... 210

CBT and Yoga.. 211

Well-being in the Workplace 212

Tips to get technology working in support of yourself 215

Chapter 12 - Guilt 217

What Is Guilt? 218

Guilt Psychology..219

Kinds of Guilt 220

Various sources can add to the guilt 222

    Family 222

    Culture.. 222

    Religious Beliefs 223

    Society 223

Impacts of Guilt... 224

Physical Symptoms of Guilt... 225

Conclusion 227

Introduction

Cognitive-behavioral therapy (CBT) is a type of psychological treatment that has been exhibited to be viable for a range of issues, including misery, nervousness issues, alcohol, and medication use issues, marital issues, dietary issues, and severe mental illness. Various research contemplates proposing that CBT prompts noteworthy improvement in working and personal satisfaction. In numerous investigations, CBT is as powerful as, or more compelling than, different types of mental treatment or psychiatric medications.

Emphasize that propels in CBT have been made based on both research and clinical practice. In reality, CBT is a methodology for scientific evidence that the strategies that have been grown produce change. As such, CBT varies from numerous different types of psychological treatment.

CBT depends on a few core standards, including:

Psychological issues are based, to some extent, on flawed or unhelpful methods of thinking.

Psychological issues are based, to some degree, on learned patterns of unhelpful behavior.

People experiencing psychological issues can learn better

methods of adapting to them, in this manner, alleviating their side effects and getting progressively viable in their lives.

CBT treatment includes endeavors to change thinking patterns. These methodologies may include:

- It is figuring out how to perceive one's mutilations in feelings that are making issues and afterward to rethink them considering reality.

- I am gaining better comprehension of the conduct and inspiration of others.

- I am using critical thinking aptitudes to adapt to troublesome situations.

- Learning to build up a more prominent feeling of certainty is one's capacities.

CBT treatment generally includes endeavors to change behavioral patterns. These procedures may include:

- They were confronting one's apprehensions as opposed to abstaining from them.

- I am using pretending to get ready for conceivably tricky cooperation's with others.

- Learning to quiet one's mind and loosen up one's body.

Not all CBT will utilize these strategies. Or maybe, the therapist and patient/client cooperate, in a shared pattern, to build up a comprehension of the issue and a treatment strategy.

CBT places an accentuation on helping people figure out how to be their therapists. Through activities in the meeting just as "schoolwork" practices outside of meetings, patients/clients are assisted in creating adapting skills, whereby they can figure out how to change their thinking, problematic feelings, and conduct.

CBT therapists accentuate what is happening in the individual's present life, as opposed to what has paved the way to their troubles. A specific amount of information about one's history is required, yet the emphasis is principally on pushing ahead to grow progressively effective ways of adapting to life.

The History of Cognitive Behavioral Therapy

Cognitive-behavioral therapy was imagined by a psychiatrist, Aaron Beck, during the 1960s. He was doing psychoanalysis at that point and saw that during his expository meetings, his patients would, in general, have an internal dialogue going on in their brains—as though they were conversing with themselves. But, they would just report a fraction of this sort of speculation to him.

For instance, in a therapy session, the client may be pondering internally: "He (the therapist) hasn't said a lot of today. I wonder if he's irritated with me?" These thoughts may cause the client to feel somewhat restless or maybe irritated. The individual could then react to this idea with a further idea: "He's presumably worn out, or maybe I haven't been discussing the most significant things." The hesitation may change how the client was feeling.

Beck understood that the connection between thoughts and feelings was significant. He created the term "automatic thoughts" to depict emotion-filled thoughts that may fly off in mind. Beck found that individuals weren't completely aware of such contemplations in every case, yet could figure out how to recognize and report them. If an individual was feeling disturbed somehow or another, the thoughts were normally negative and neither reasonable nor supportive. Beck found that distinguishing these thoughts was the way into the client's understanding and beating their troubles.

Beck called it cognitive therapy, given the significance it puts on speculation. It's presently known as cognitive-behavioral therapy (CBT) because the treatment utilizes behavior procedures also. The balance between the cognitive and the social components fluctuates among the various treatments of this sort. However, it totally goes under the umbrella term cognitive behavior therapy. CBT has since experienced successful scientific trials in numerous spots by various groups and has been applied to a wide variety of issues.

What Does CBT Treatment Resemble?

Cognitive-behavioral therapy differs from numerous psychotherapies since meetings have a structure, as opposed to the individual speaking unreservedly about whatever rings a bell. Toward the start of the treatment, the client meets the therapist to portray explicit issues and set objectives they need to progress. The issues might be troublesome side effects, such as resting badly, not having the option to associate with companions, or trouble focusing on reading or work. Or then again, they could be life issues, for example, being unhappy at work, experiencing difficulty managing an adolescent child, or being in a miserable marriage.

At that point, these issues and objectives become the reason for arranging the content of meetings and examining how to manage them. Regularly, toward the start of a session, the client and therapist will mutually settle on the primary subjects they need to work away this week. They will permit time to talk about the conclusions from the last session. Furthermore, they will look at the advancement made with the schoolwork the client set for oneself last time. Toward the finish of the session, they will design another task to do outside the sessions.

Doing Homework

Taking a shot at schoolwork assignments between meetings is a fundamental piece of the procedure. What this may include will change. For instance, toward the beginning of the treatment, the specialist may request that the client keep a diary of any occurrences that incite a feeling of anxiety or depression, with the goal that they can look at thoughts encompassing the incident. Later on in the treatment, another task may comprise of activities to adapt to issue circumstances of a specific kind.

The significance of the structure

The purpose behind having this structure is that it assists in utilizing the therapeutic time most proficiently. It ensures that significant information isn't passed up a great opportunity (the consequences of the schoolwork, for example) and that both therapist and client consider new assignments that normally follow from the meeting.

The therapist takes a functioning part in organizing the sessions in any case. As progress is made, and clients handle the standards, they find supportive, and they take more duty regarding the content of sessions increasingly. So by the end, the client feels enabled to keep working freely.

Group sessions

Cognitive-behavioral therapy is typically one-to-one therapy. But on the other hand, it's appropriate to working in groups or families, especially toward the start of treatment. Numerous individuals discover incredible profit by offering their troubles to other people who may have comparable issues, even though this may appear to be overwhelming from the outset. The group can be a wellspring of particularly important help and guidance since it originates from individuals with personal experience of an issue. By observing a few people immediately, the service providers can offer assistance to more individuals simultaneously, so individuals get help sooner.

How else does it vary from different therapies?

Cognitive-behavioral therapy additionally varies from different treatments in the idea of the relationship that the therapist will attempt to set up. A few treatments urge the client to be subject to the advisor as a component of the treatment procedure. The client can then effortlessly come to consider the therapist as all-knowing and all-powerful. The relationship is diverse with CBT.

CBT favors a progressively equivalent relationship that may be more business-like, being issue engaged and pragmatic. The therapist will regularly approach the client for feedback and their perspectives on what is happening in therapy. Beck authored the term 'collaborative empiricism', which stresses the significance of client and therapist cooperating in trying out how the thoughts behind CBT may apply to the client's circumstance and issues.

Who Benefits from Trying CBT?

Individuals who portray having specific issues are frequently the most reasonable for CBT because it works through having a particular concentration and objectives. It might be less appropriate for somebody who feels enigmatically sad or unfulfilled, yet who doesn't have alarming side effects or a specific part of their life they need to take a shot at.

It's probably going to be progressively useful for any individual who can identify with CBT's ideas, its problem-solving approach, and the requirement for practical self-assignments. Individuals will, in general, lean toward CBT if they need a progressively viable treatment, where gaining knowledge isn't the fundamental point.

CBT can be an effective therapy for the accompanying issues:

- Anger management

- Anxiety and panic attacks

- Child and adolescent issues

- Chronic fatigue syndrome

- Chronic pain

- Depression

- Medication or alcohol issues

- Eating issues

- General medical issues

- Propensities, for example, facial tics

- Mood swings

- Obsessive-compulsive disorder

- Fears

- Post-traumatic stress disorder

- Sexual and relationship issues

- Sleep issues

There is another and quickly developing enthusiasm for utilizing CBT (along with drug) with individuals who experience the ill effects of mind flights and dreams, and those with long term issues in identifying with others.

It's less simple to take care of issues that are all the more seriously disabling and all the more long-standing through short-term therapy. In any case, individuals can regularly learn rules that improve their satisfaction and increment their chances of gaining further ground. There is a wide variety of self-help literature. It gives information about medicines to specific issues and thoughts regarding what individuals can do on their own or with loved ones.

Chapter 1 - Cognitive distortions

A significant number of the most famous and effective cognitive-behavioral therapy techniques are applied to what psychologists call "cognitive distortions," erroneous contemplations that strengthen negative idea patterns or feelings.

15 primary cognitive distortions can plague even the most balanced thinkers.

1. Filtering

Filtering alludes to how an individual can overlook the entirety of the positive and beneficial things in life to concentrate exclusively on the negative. It's the trap of dwelling on a single negative part of a circumstance, even when encircled by a wealth of beneficial things.

2. Polarized Thinking/Black-and-White Thinking

This cognitive distortion is all-or-nothing thinking, with no space for unpredictability or subtlety—everything's either black or white, never shades of gray.

If you don't perform impeccably in some area, at that point, you may consider yourself to be an all-out disappointment rather than perceiving that you might be unskilled in one area.

3. Overgeneralization

Overgeneralization is taking a single occurrence or point in time and utilizing it as the sole piece of evidence for a wide end.

For instance, somebody who overgeneralizes could bomb a significant job interview. As opposed to forgetting about it as one bad experience and attempting again, they presume that they are terrible at talking and will never find a new line of a work offer.

4. Jumping to Conclusions

Like overgeneralization, this distortion includes flawed thinking in how one makes conclusions. Dissimilar to overgeneralizing one incident, making conclusions alludes to the propensity to make certain of something with no evidence at all.

For instance, we may be persuaded that somebody detests us without any genuine proof. We may accept that our fears will work out as expected before we get an opportunity to discover the truth.

5. Catastrophizing/Magnifying or Minimizing

This distortion includes expecting that the most exceedingly terrible will occur or has occurred, in light of an occurrence that is not even close as disastrous as it is described. For instance, you may commit a little error at work and be persuaded that it will demolish the project you are working on, that your supervisor will be furious, and that you'll lose your employment.

Then again, one may limit the significance of positive things, such as achievement at work or attractive personal characteristics.

6. Personalization

This is where an individual accepts that all they do affects external events or others, regardless of how unreasonable they might be. An individual with this distortion will feel that the person in question has an overstated role in the bad things that occur around them.

For example, an individual may accept that showing up a couple of moments late to a meeting prompted it to be crashed and that everything would have been fine if they were on time.

7. Control Fallacies

These distortions include feeling like everything that transpires is either an aftereffect of simply outer powers or totally because of your activities. Sometimes what occurs is because of forces we can't control, and now and then what it's because of our activities. However, the distortion is accepting that it is consistently either.

We may accept that difficult associates are at fault for our own not exactly heavenly work, or then again expect that every mistake another person makes is a direct result of something we did.

8. Fallacy of Fairness

We are regularly worried about fairness; however, this worry can be taken to boundaries. As we as a whole know, life isn't in every case reasonable. The individual who experiences life searching for fairness in the entirety of their encounters will wind up angry and troubled.

Now and again, things will go our direction, and in some cases, they won't, paying little heed to how reasonable it might appear.

9. Blaming

When things don't go our way, there are numerous ways we can clarify or allot obligation regarding the result. One method for appointing obligation is reprimanding others for what turns out badly.

Now and again, we may blame others for causing us to feel or act a specific way; however, this is a cognitive distortion. Just you are answerable for how you feel or act.

10. "Shoulds."

"Shoulds" allude to the implicit or explicit principles we have about how we and others ought to carry on. When others disrupt our norms, we are disturbed. When we disrupt our norms, we feel remorseful. For instance, we may have an informal guideline that client service representatives ought to be pleasing to the client consistently.

When we connect with a client service representative that isn't quickly pleasing, we may blow up. If we have an implicit rule that we are reckless if we burn through cash on extra things, we may feel exceedingly remorseful when we spend even a small amount of cash on something we needn't bother with.

11. Emotional Reasoning

This distortion includes imagining that if we feel a specific way, it must be valid. For instance, if we feel ugly or uninteresting in the present second, we think we are ugly or uninteresting. This cognitive distortion comes down to:

"I feel it; therefore, it must be valid."

Unmistakably, our feelings are not generally characteristic of the goal truth; however, it tends to be hard to look past how we feel.

12. Fallacy of Change

The fallacy of change lies in anticipating that others should change as it suits us. This ties into the inclination that our happiness relies upon others, and their reluctance or failure to change, regardless of whether we request it, shields us from being upbeat.

This is a harming approach to think because nobody is answerable for our joy, aside from ourselves.

13. Global Labeling/Mislabeling

This cognitive distortion is an extraordinary type of summing up, wherein we sum one up or two instances or characteristics into a worldwide judgment. For instance, if we come up short at a particular task, we may infer that we are a complete disappointment here as well as all areas.

Then again, when a more stranger says something somewhat inconsiderate, we may presume that the individual in question is unpleasant in general. Mislabeling is explicit to utilizing misrepresented and genuinely stacked language, for example, saying a lady has relinquished her kids when she leaves her children with a babysitter to enjoy a night out.

14. Continually Being Right

While we as a whole appreciate being right, these distortions make us figure we should be correct, that being off-base is unsatisfactory.

We may accept that being correct is a higher priority than the feelings of others, having the option to concede when we've committed a mistake or being reasonable and objective.

15. Heaven's Reward Fallacy

These distortions include expecting that any sacrifice or abstinence will pay off. We may think about this karma and expect that karma will, in every case, quickly reward us for our great deeds—this outcome in feelings of harshness when we don't get our reward.

Numerous tools and techniques found in cognitive behavioral therapy are planned to address or opposite these cognitive distortions.

Essential CBT Techniques and Tools

There are numerous techniques and tools utilized in cognitive behavioral therapy, a large number of which can be utilized in both a treatment setting and in regular day to day existence. The nine techniques and tools listed below are probably the most widely recognized and viable CBT practices.

1. Journaling

This technique is an approach to assemble one's mood and thoughts. A CBT journal can incorporate the hour of the disposition or thought, its wellspring, the degree or intensity, and how we responded, among different components.

This procedure can assist us in identifying our thought patterns and emotional inclinations, depict them, and change, adjust, or adapt to them.

2. Unraveling Cognitive Distortions

This is an essential objective of CBT and can be drilled with or without the assistance of a therapist. To unwind cognitive distortions, you should initially get mindful of the distortions from which you ordinarily endure.

Some portion of this includes distinguishing and challenging harmful automatic thoughts, which often can be categorized as one of the 15 categories as listed before.

3. Cognitive Restructuring

When you recognize the distortions you hold, you can start to investigate how those distortions flourished and why you came to trust them. When you find a belief that is dangerous or hurtful, you can start to challenge it.

For instance, if you accept that you should have a high paying to be a decent individual, you will start to feel awful about yourself at that point laid off from your high-paying job.

Rather than tolerating this faulty belief that drives you to negative thoughts, you could accept an open the door to consider what truly makes an individual "respectable," a belief you might not have unequivocally considered previously.

4. Exposure and Response Prevention

This technique is explicitly powerful for the individuals who experience from obsessive-compulsive disorder (OCD). You can practice this procedure by presenting yourself to whatever it is that regularly evokes a compulsive behavior, yet putting forth a valiant effort to refrain from the behavior.

You can consolidate journaling with this technique, or use journaling to see how this technique causes you to feel.

5. Interoceptive Exposure

This technique is expected to treat frenzy and tension. It includes exposure to dreaded bodily sensations to evoke the reaction. Doing so initiates any unhelpful beliefs related to the sensations, keeps up the sensations without interruption or evasion, and permits new finding out about the sensations to happen.

It is proposed to enable the victim to see that frenzy side effects are not dangerous, although they might be uncomfortable.

6. Nightmare Exposure and Rescripting

Nightmare exposure and rescripting are expected explicitly for those suffering from nightmares. This procedure is like interoceptive exposure, in that the bad dream is inspired, which raises the relevant emotion.

When the feeling has emerged, the client and therapist cooperate to recognize the ideal feeling and build up another picture to go with the desired emotion.

7. Play the Script Until the End

This technique is particularly valuable for those experiencing fear and tension. In this technique, the person who is powerless against devastating apprehension or tension directs a kind of psychological study wherein they envision the result of the worst-case scenario.

Letting this situation play out can assist the person in recognizing that even if the person fears happens, the result will, in any case, be manageable.

8. Progressive Muscle Relaxation

This is a recognizable technique to the individuals who practice care. Like the body filter, this technique teaches you to loosen up each muscle group in turn until your entire body is in a condition of unwinding.

You can utilize audio guidance, a YouTube video, or essentially your brain to practice this technique, and it tends to be particularly useful for quieting nerves and mitigating an occupied and unfocused mind.

9. Relaxed Breathing

This is another technique that will be natural to practitioners of mindfulness. There are numerous approaches to unwind and carry consistency to your breath, including guided and unguided imagery, audio recordings, YouTube recordings, and contents. Carrying consistency and quiet to your breath will permit you to move toward your issues from a parity position, encouraging increasingly successful and rational decisions.

These techniques can help those experiencing a range of mental illnesses and distresses, including anxiety, sadness, OCD, and panic disorder, and they can be practiced with or without the direction of a therapist.

CBT Interventions and Exercises

Haven't you had enough CBT tools yet? Peruse on for extra helpful and successful activities.

1. Behavioral Experiments

These are identified with psychological studies, in that you take part in an "imagine a scenario in which" thought. Behavioral experiments vary from psychological studies in that you try out these "what uncertainties" outside of your considerations.

To test a thought, you can explore different avenues regarding the results that various contemplations produce. For instance, you can test the thoughts:

"If I censure myself, I will be motivated to work more diligently" versus "If I am benevolent to myself, I will be spurred to work more enthusiastically."

In the first place, you would have a go at condemning yourself when you need the inspiration to work more diligently and record the outcomes. At that point, you would take a stab at being benevolent to yourself and recording the outcomes. Next, you would contrast the outcomes with see which thought was nearer to reality.

These Behavioral Experiments to Test Beliefs can assist you in figuring out how to accomplish your important objectives and how to be your best self.

2. Thought Records

Thought records are valuable in testing the validity of your thoughts. They include assembling and assessing proof for and against a specific idea, taking into account a proof put together end concerning whether the idea is legitimate or not.

For instance, you may believe, "My companion believes I'm a terrible companion." You would think about all the proof for this conviction, for example, "She didn't pick up the telephone the last time I called," or "She dropped our arrangements ultimately." And proof against this conviction, similar to "She got back to me after not picking up the telephone," and "She welcomed me to her grill one week from now. If she thought I was a bad companion, she presumably wouldn't have invited me."

When you have evidence for and against, the goal is to concocted increasingly adjusted contemplations. For example, "My companion is occupied and has different companions, so she can't generally pick up the telephone when I call. If I am incomprehension of this, I will genuinely be a good friend."

Thought records apply the utilization of logic to avoid preposterous negative contemplations and supplant them with increasingly adjusted, rational thoughts.

3. Pleasant Activity Scheduling

This technique can be particularly useful for managing depression. It includes planning exercises sooner rather than later that you can anticipate.

For instance, you may record one action for every day that you will take part throughout the following week. This can be as straightforward as viewing a film you are eager to see or calling a companion to visit. It very well may be whatever is charming for you, as long as it isn't undesirable (i.e., eating an entire cake at a time or smoking).

You can have scheduling activity for every day that gives you a feeling of dominance or achievement. It's incredible to accomplish something wonderful, yet accomplishing something little that can cause you to feel achieved may have all the more dependable and broad impacts.

This basic technique can bring greater inspiration into your life, and our Pleasant Activity Scheduling Worksheet is intended to help.

4. Imagery Based Exposure

This activity includes contemplating an ongoing memory that delivered strong negative feelings and breaking down the situation.

For instance, if you recently had a fight with your loved one, and they said something frightful, you can carry that situation to mind and attempt to recollect it in detail. Next, you would attempt to name the feelings and thoughts you encountered during the circumstance and distinguish the urges you felt (e.g., to run away, to shout at your better half, or to cry).

Envisioning this negative circumstance, particularly for a drawn-out timeframe, can assist you in taking endlessly its capacity to trigger you and lessen evasion adapting. When you open yourself to the entirety of the feelings and urges you felt in the circumstance and endure encountering the memory, it removes a portion of its capacity.

5. Graded Exposure Worksheet

This technique may sound confused, yet it's moderately straightforward.

Making a circumstance introduction pecking order implies posting circumstances that you would typically avoid. For instance, somebody with extreme social anxiety may ordinarily abstain from making a call or asking somebody out on the town.

Next, you rate everything on how upset you figure you would be, on a scale from 0 to 10, if you are occupied with it. For the individual experiencing serious social tension, asking somebody out on the date might be appraised a 10 on the scale, while making a call may be evaluated more like a 3 or 4.

When you have evaluated the situations, you rank them as per their misery rating. This will assist you in perceiving the greatest challenges you face, which can help you choose which things to address and what request. It's frequently encouraged to begin with the least upsetting things and stir your way up to the most troubling things.

5 Final Cognitive Behavioral Activities

Before we go, there are a couple of more CBT exercises and activities that might be useful for you or your clients that we'd prefer to cover.

1. Mindfulness Meditation

Mindfulness can have a wide scope of positive effects, incorporating assisting in sadness, nervousness, compulsion, and numerous other psychological illnesses or challenges.

Mindfulness can help those experiencing hurtful automatic thoughts to withdraw from rumination and fixation by helping them remain solidly grounded in the present.

2. Progressive Approximation

This is an extravagant name for a straightforward thought that you have likely previously known: separating enormous errands into little advances.

It very well may be overpowering to be confronted with a huge goal, such as starting a business or rebuilding a house. This is also valid in emotional well-being treatment, since the objective of conquering depression or anxiety and accomplishing mental well-being can appear to be an amazing assignment.

By breaking the enormous objective into little, simple to-achieve steps, we can outline the way to progress and cause the excursion to appear to be somewhat less overpowering.

3. Keeping in touch with Self-Statements to Counteract Negative Thoughts

This method can be hard for somebody new to CBT treatment or experiencing serious indications, yet it can be very successful.

When negative thoughts are tormenting you (or your client), it tends to be difficult to defy them, particularly if your confidence in these thoughts is strong. To neutralize these negative musings, it very well may be useful to record a positive, inverse idea.

For instance, if the idea "I am useless" continues flying into your head, take a stab at recording an announcement like "I am an individual with worth," or "I am an individual with potential." Before all else, it tends to be hard to acknowledge these substitution contemplations, yet the more you draw out these positive thoughts to check the negative ones, the more grounded the affiliation will be.

4. Imagine the Best Parts of Your Day

When you are feeling discouraged or negative, it is hard to perceive that there are sure parts of life. This straightforward strategy of inferring the great pieces of your day can be a little advance toward perceiving the positive.

You should simply record the things throughout your life that you are appreciative of or the best occasions that occur on a given day. The basic demonstration of writing down these beneficial things can fashion new associations in your mind that make it simpler to see the positive if you encounter negative feelings.

5. Reframe Your Negative Thoughts

It very well may be anything but difficult to surrender to negative thoughts as a default setting. If you wind up promptly thinking a negative idea when you see something new, for example, going into a new room and thinking, "I abhor the color of that wall," check out reframing.

Reframing includes countering the negative thought(s) by seeing things you feel positive about as fast as could be expected under the circumstances. For example, in the model where you promptly consider the amount you hate the color of that wall, you would drive yourself to see five things in the room that you feel about (e.g., the floor carpets look comfortable, the lampshade is beautiful, the windows let in a great deal of daylight).

You can set your telephone to remind you of the day to stop what you are doing and think about the positive things around you. This can assist you in pushing your thoughts once more into the realm of the positive rather than the negative.

6. A Take-Home Message

We offered numerous techniques, tools, and resources that can be powerful in the battle against wretchedness, anxiety, OCD, and a large group of different issues or challenges.

However, similar to the case with numerous medicines, they rely upon you (or your client) investing in a ton of energy. We urge you to give these procedures a genuine attempt to permit yourself the advantage of thinking that they could work.

When we approach a potential arrangement with the suspicion that it won't work, that supposition regularly turns into an inevitable outcome. When we approach a potential arrangement with an open mind and the belief that it very well might work, it has a greatly improved possibility of succeeding.

So if you are struggling with negative automatic thoughts, if it's not too much trouble, consider these tips and techniques and give them a shot. In like manner, if your client is struggling, urging them to put forth the attempt, because the result can be better than they can envision.

Chapter 2 - Raise your self-esteem

Low self-esteem implies not having a favorable opinion of yourself as an individual, or not holding yourself in high respect. If you have low confidence, you probably won't feel sure or skilled, may feel anxious, and may condemn yourself harshly. Psychologists imagine that underneath feelings of low self-esteem are the negative beliefs and assessments we hold about ourselves. A few people realize that their contrary judgment of themselves is excessively brutal, others clutch these beliefs so unequivocally that they can feel like realities. Luckily, there are useful psychological approaches for improving your self-esteem.

How is it to have low self-esteem?

Daniel's belief that he was useless and different

Daniel was the youngest of four kids. Growing up, he cherished comic books and film, and he proceeded to contemplate filmmaking at school. Scholastically he wasn't as brilliant as his sisters, something he felt his folks blamed him for. Daniel had a little group of friends, yet he was additionally tormented at school. He came to accept that he was dumb, 'different,' and useless. He would get bothered when encircled by individuals he thought of as increasingly capable, never felt agreeable around women, and never felt like fit in. Daniel turned out to be extremely self-critical. He believed he must be watching out for his imperfections to attempt to conceal them from others before they took note.

Parts of treatment that Daniel discovered accommodating

Daniel thought it was useful to think about his negative beliefs as an opinion instead of reality and comprehend where this conclusion had originated from. The piece of treatment that he discovered most accommodating was the point at which his specialist acquainted him with testing his critical voice. It felt unusual in the first place; however, he quickly started to see that his feeling of uselessness had no premise. He had left school and had begun college, which gave him the opportunity to explore different avenues regarding demonstrating sides of his character that he hadn't felt OK with previously: meeting individuals with comparable interests helped him to grasp his 'difference' as a positive trait lastly begin to feel great in his skin.

What is low self-esteem?

Your self-esteem is simply the opinion you have of yourself. When you have healthy self-esteem, you will, in general, contemplate yourself, about existence by and large. When you experience difficulties, you feel sure that you will be capable of facing them. Individuals with strong confidence realize that they are significant and will name probably some of their positive attributes, for example, "I am a good friend," "I am thoughtful," "I am honest," or "I am a good father."

When you have low self-esteem, you will observe yourself, the world, and your future all the more adversely and critically. When you experience difficulties, you question whether you will have the option to ascend to them, and you may avoid them. You may converse with yourself cruelly in your brain, for example, letting yourself know, "You're moronic," "You'll never deal with this," or "I don't add up to anything." You may feel on edge, tragic, low, or unmotivated.

No one is brought into the world with low self-esteem – it creates because of the experiences we have for the duration of our lives. At the center of low self-esteem are simply the convictions and feelings we hold about ourselves. We disclose to ourselves tales about what our identity is and structure decisions about ourselves. These opinions can get 'fixed,' just as they are 'truths' forever. As a general rule, however, they are simply stories or marks, and they don't catch the full truth of our identity.

What causes low self-esteem?

Negative early experiences are significant for the improvement of low self-esteem. A portion of the components that make it more probable that an individual will grow low self-esteem include:

<u>Early experiences, including discipline, disregard, or abuse</u>. Early experiences, for example, abuse, disregard, harassing, or punishment, are significant. Children who endure these sorts of experiences regularly, structure the belief that they are bad and more likely than not merited the discipline.

<u>You are neglecting to meet others' expectations</u>. You may feel that you are bad enough since you neglected to meet another person's expectations–this may have implied your parent's unrealistic standards–note this doesn't imply that the expectations were fair or adjusted in any case.

<u>Neglecting to fulfill the standards of your peer group</u>. Being unique or the 'odd one out' during adolescence, when your character is framing, can capably affect your self-esteem.

<u>They are not getting enough warmth, fondness, applause, love, or encouragement</u>. It is conceivable to grow low self-esteem even without clear negative encounters, yet simply through a

deficiency of positive ones. Without enough support that we are acceptable, exceptional, or cherished, kids can shape the feeling that they are sufficiently bad.

Build self-esteem

Self-esteem is a term that truly alludes to how we consider ourselves. One might say, it is the total of the entirety of the contemplations that go through our head when pondering our confidence in our capacities. When individuals talk about good self-esteem, what they're truly discussing is a sound degree of self-confidence. Poor self-esteem then again has to do with extreme self-confidence. Poor self-esteem can bring about anxiety and depression. Cognitive-behavioral therapy is the most examined treatment demonstrated to be powerful in helping build self-esteem.

Cognitive-behavioral therapy is the treatment of decision for most mental issues. It is intended to be brief, problem-focused, and dynamic. Instead of concentrating on early developmental history and relationships, cognitive behavioral therapy focuses on the issues that are happening in the present. Cognitive-behavioral therapy for low self-esteem may incorporate a mix of the accompanying treatments:

<u>Cognitive restructuring</u>: Cognitive restructuring is a combination of perceiving unhelpful reasoning patterns and supplanting them with progressively viable thinking patterns. Cognitive restructuring for low self-esteem regularly centers on recognizing negative thoughts about oneself and distinguishing distorted thinking, for example, marking oneself as a failure because of one aptitude shortfall or negative event.

<u>Behavioral activation</u>: When individuals have low self-esteem, they regularly dodge exercises and circumstances that they dread, they won't do well in. Subsequently, they have not many open doors for compensating encounters and regularly become discouraged. Behavioral activation inverts this cycle by helping individuals reconnect with life, and subsequently have all the more rewarding experiences.

<u>Assertiveness training</u>: People with poor self-esteem frequently experience issues requesting what they need, disapproving solicitations, or expressing their actual emotions. Assertiveness training is a method of helping individuals figure out how to successfully and handily get what they need from others without relinquishing their relationships.

<u>Problem-solving training</u>: When individuals have had low self-esteem over an extensive time, they will, in general, feel defenseless. Problem-solving training assists individuals in finding a feeling of agency by instructing them to perceive issues, distinguish resources and potential arrangements, and,

lastly, complete, compelling plans.

<u>Social skills training</u>: Low self-esteem is frequently interwoven with social abilities deficits. Social skills training assists individuals in expanding positive and remunerating social practices and diminishing negative social behavior, such as complaining.

8 Steps to Improving Your Self-Esteem

With regards to your self-esteem, just one opinion matters—your own. What's more, even that one ought to be deliberately assessed, we will, in general, be our own harshest critics.

"Unrestricted human worth expect that every one of us is brought into the world with all the limits expected to live productively, although everybody has a different mix of abilities, which are at various degrees of improvement." He emphasizes that center worth is free of externals that the marketplace values, such as riches, training, well-being, status—or how one has been dealt with.

Explore the world—and relationships—scanning for any piece of proof to approve their self-constraining beliefs. Much like adjudicator and jury, they continually put themselves being investigated and, at times, sentence themselves to a lifetime of self-criticism.

The following are eight steps you can take to expand your feelings of self-worth.

1. Be careful.

We can't change something if we don't perceive that there is something to change. By just getting aware of our negative self-talk, we start to remove ourselves from the emotions it raises. This empowers us to relate to them less. Without this mindfulness, we can undoubtedly fall into the snare of accepting our self-limiting talk, and as medication teacher Allan Lokos says, "Don't think all that you think. Thoughts are only that — thoughts."

When you wind up going down the way of self-criticism, tenderly note what's going on, be interested in it, and remind yourself, "These are thoughts, not realities."

2. Change the story.

As a whole, we have a narrative or a story we've made about ourselves that shapes our self-recognition; after that, our core self-image is based. If we need to change that story, we need to comprehend where it originated from and where we got the messages we let ourselves know. Whose voices would we say we are internalizing?

"Once in a while automatic negative thoughts like 'you're fat' or 'you're languid' can be practiced in your mind so frequently that you begin to accept they are valid," "These thoughts are found out, which implies they can be unlearned. You can begin with assertions. What do you wish you accepted about yourself? Repeat these phrases to yourself consistently."

Familiarity preparing" in positive attestations (for instance, recording the same number of various positive things you can about yourself in a moment) can reduce side effects of depression as estimated without anyone else report utilizing the Beck Depression Inventory. Larger quantities of composed, positive explanations have corresponded with more prominent improvement.

3. Abstain from falling into the look at the and-despair rabbit hole.

"Two key things I accentuate are to practice acknowledgment and quit contrasting yourself with others." "I accentuation that since another person seems happy on social media or even face to face doesn't mean they are cheerful. Comparisons just lead to negative self-talk, which prompts tension and stress." Feelings of low self-esteem can adversely influence your emotional well-being just as different zones throughout your life, for example, work, relationships, and physical well-being.

4. Channel your inner rock star.

"Everyone is a genius. In any case, but if you judge a fish by its ability to climb a tree, it will carry on with as long as it can remember accepting that it is moronic." We all have our strengths and weaknesses. Somebody might be a splendid artist, however, a dreadful cook. Neither one of the qualities characterizes their center worth. Perceive what your qualities are and the sentiments of certainty they cause, particularly amid uncertainty. It's anything but difficult to make speculations when you "mess up" or "fail" at something; however, helping yourself remember the manners in which your rock offers an increasingly realistic point of view of yourself.

Was there a period in your life where you would be advised to self-esteem? What were you doing at that phase of your life?" If it's hard for you to distinguish your unique gifts, request that a companion bring them up to you. Sometimes it's simpler for others to see the best in us than it is for us to see it in ourselves.

5. Exercise.

Numerous investigations have demonstrated a correlation between activity and higher confidence, just as improved emotional well-being. "Practicing makes strengthening both physical and mental," "particularly weight lifting where you can adjust the achievements. Exercise sorts out your day around self-care." She recommends dropping an undertaking every day from your unending daily plan for the sole motivation behind unwinding or accomplishing something fun, and perceiving how that feels. Different types of self-care, such as proper nutrition and sufficient sleep, have appeared to positively affect one's self-discernment.

6. Do unto others.

Hershenson recommends electing to help individuals who might be less fortunate. "Being of service to others helps remove you from your head. When you can help another person, it makes you less centered on your issues."

"What I find is that the more somebody accomplishes something in their life that they can be pleased with, the simpler it is for them to perceive their value. Doing things that one can regard themselves is the one key that I have discovered that attempts to raise one's worth. It is something unmistakable.

Aiding at a homeless shelter, animal shelter, giving of time at an older sibling or sister association. These are things which offer an incentive to oneself, however, to another person also."

There is a lot of truth to the way that what we put out there into the world will, in general, boomerang back to us. To test this out, go through a day deliberately putting out positive thoughts and practices toward those with whom you come into contact. As you approach your day, be aware of what returns to you, and notice if your state of mind improves.

7. Forgiveness

Is someone a major part of your life you haven't forgiven? A family member? A relative? Yourself? By clutching feelings of harshness or hatred, we keep ourselves stuck in a pattern of antagonism. If we haven't pardoned ourselves, disgrace will keep us in this same loop.

"Forgiving oneself, as well as other people, has been found to develop self-esteem, "maybe because it associates us with our intrinsically cherishing nature and advances an acknowledgment of individuals, regardless of our imperfections." He alludes to the Buddhist meditation on forgiveness, which can be drilled whenever: "If I have harmed or hurt anybody, consciously or unconsciously, I ask forgiveness. If anybody has harmed or hurt me, intentionally or unintentionally, I excuse them. For the manners in which I have harmed myself, intentionally or unintentionally, I offer forgiveness."

8. Recollect that you are not your circumstances

At long last, figuring out how to differentiate between your circumstances and what your identity is critical to self-worth. "Perceiving internal worth, and loving one's flawed self, give the safe establishment to development. "With that security, one is allowed to develop with pleasure, not fear of failure—because that failure doesn't change center worth."

We are brought into the world with unbounded potential and equivalent worth as individuals. We are anything less is a deception that we have learned after some time. Consequently, with difficult work and self-compassion, self-destructive thoughts and convictions can be unlearned. Making the steps outlined above is a beginning in the push to expand self-esteem and to "perceive self-esteem. It exists in every individual."

Chapter 3 - Transform your mentality

If you've been in the market for a psychological wellness supplier, you've presumably run over references to "cognitive behavioral therapy" or "Cognitive therapy," as these are regular methodologies for treating an assortment of emotional well-being conditions, including sorrow and nervousness. Comprehensively, cognitive therapies show clients how to function with, oversee, or change their thoughts to decrease manifestations, for example, discouraged state of mind, stress, a sleeping disorder, and so forth. The idea here is that when you can oversee or change your thoughts to be less troubling, you'll feel better genuinely and take part in healthy behaviors.

This bodes well to the vast majority, yet many clients grumble to me that a portion of the methods prescribed to them to move their thoughts appear to be silly, shallow, or too tricky feely. I'll hear, "My last therapist instructed me to rehash these useless insistences..." Or, "I laughed when my therapist instructed me to write in red lipstick on my bathroom mirror, what an adorable individual I am..." Often, these "think positive" sorts of activities are viewed as an exercise in futility. For what reason would therapists suggest this stuff? What is going in the brain during cognitive therapy and, all the more explicitly, for what reason it would be a good idea for us to participate in the corny thought-shifting techniques promoted by the certain therapists and New Age thinkers?

The appropriate response, set forth plainly, is that when we take part in cognitive therapy, including a wide range of cognitive rebuilding and thought-shifting techniques, we change critical neural networks that shape how we think, feel, and see the world, just as what we accept to be conceivable.

The mind contains approximately 86 billion neurons, every one of which is associated with around 10,000 others. The associations between these neurons sort out themselves as indicated by points, or topics, and become neural networks after some time. The outcome is that we have billions of neural networks devoted to a wide range of considerations, themes, feelings, and situations. For instance, we as a whole have a neural network called "dogs," "the color white," "coffee," and so on. If you've at any point concentrated on it, you likely have a neural system for it. To comprehend why intellectual treatment can be so useful, it's helpful to see some essential rules about how neural networks work. Here are the three main rules of neural networks:

The Three Rules of Neural Networks

<u>1. The focal point of your consideration is the network you are in</u>. If you are contemplating cleaning your toilet, you are in that network as long as you continue concentrating on that point. If you're reflecting what a good or bad individual you will be, you are in the "good person" or "bad person" network so long as your brain is centered on that subject. Your attention discloses to you the neural network you are in. While it is entirely expected to get ourselves mysteriously in some old network's profundities that may not be useful, we can figure out how to practice mindful awareness to start seeing where the brain meanders and lands. Furthermore, when required, we can start to move regard for increasingly helpful networks.

<u>2. Neurons that fire together wire together</u>. This is called Hebb's Rule (1949), which fundamentally says that rehashed experience can strengthen or debilitate neuronal bonds. The more neurons fire together, the quicker and more grounded they wire together, creating bigger and more grounded organizes after some time. This means when you invest a ton of energy in a specific system (which means you're concentrating on one thing a great deal), you develop it, and it expands and more grounded.

There's a New Age development going on, which discloses to us that what we think about can develop, and thoughts can turn out to be genuine. A few people even accept that with musings, they can "manifest" certain results in their lives. While this kind of thinking welcomes eye moves from some logically disapproved of people, these ideas are supported by neuroscience. What you consider indeed develops—truly—in mind. What's more, the more you center around something, the more associations with that thing you make, which implies that after some time, you start to see the world increasingly more through that specific network/lens and the things that are associated with it. What you center around, you get much more of. To draw in with your thoughts wisely, and focus on which systems you invest a ton of energy in!

3. <u>Use it or lose it</u>. Similarly, as taking care of a specific idea reinforces the neural network related to that idea, disregarding neural networks brings about a debilitating of those systems after some time. An extraordinary case of this is a neural guide of a town. If you've at any point lived in one place and moved, you've seen after some time that you bit by bit show signs of improvement at finding your way around the new town. It doesn't occur promptly, yet it happens over a time of months, and the purpose behind this is you assemble a neural network of that new town, which gets more grounded with time. As this neural network reinforces, in any case, you may see that your memory of how to get around your old town turns out to be progressively fluffy. When you come back to your old town years after the fact, you understand you no longer can discover your way around like you used to. This is because that system

has decayed after some time because of disregard.

With neural networks, you either use them, or you lose them! This is great news since it implies that if we can advance breaking down of old, negative, unhelpful systems, we can decrease the force and recurrence with which we produce (and experience!) the upsetting contemplations related to those networks. Rather, we can manufacture new, positive, accommodating systems to invest energy in, and reality shifts.

What These Rules Mean for Therapy

When a client is occupied with cognitive therapy, or cognitive behavioral therapy, the primary objectives are to:

1.   Help the client become mindful of the system they are in by getting mindful of their musings (which can be troublesome!)

2.   Perceive how being in that network/having that thinking is useful to them or not all that supportive

3.   Become mindful of the outcomes of investing energy in that network/engaging in with that idea

4.   Move out of that network/thought into progressively accommodating networks/thoughts when required.

When we are careful about where our attention goes, we can

create our neural networks to be progressively useful, versatile, and healthy. Furthermore, when we move away from the old, unhelpful networks that contain negative self-talk or beliefs, they start to wither away as we stop to initiate them. Therefore, while appreciation works out, thinking positive, or "manifestation" through manipulation may appear to be touchy-feely. They are particularly following what we realize mind change, as they advance neural system adjustment, however, thought moving (or, in cognitive therapy language, "cognitive reappraisal"). So whenever your therapist advises you to rehash a few affirmations or round out a day by day gratitude journal, recall that they are helping you improve your mind!

Stop Negative Thoughts: Choosing a Healthier Way of Thinking

What is healthy thinking?

Healthy thinking can instruct you to realize your thoughts—both supportive and not accommodating—influence issues or sentiments that inconvenience you. With training, you can figure out how to utilize precise thoughts that support you rather than negative considerations that debilitate you.

If you stop negative thoughts, you might be progressively ready to think about yourself and handle life's difficulties. You will feel good. Also, you might be progressively ready to keep away from or adapt to pressure, nervousness, rest issues, unwanted weight increase, or depression.

Healthy thinking includes quieting your brain and body. You can use at least one technique, and these may incorporate meditation, yoga, muscle relaxation, or guided imagery.

Cognitive-behavioral therapy, additionally called CBT, is a treatment that is frequently used to assist individuals in speculation in a healthy way. It centers on thought (intellectual) and activity (behavioral). Numerous individuals work with a therapist or an instructor to learn CBT. But, you can practice healthy thinking all alone.

How does CBT assist you in intuition in a healthy way?

CBT includes techniques that you can practice each day, so healthy thinking falls into place without a hitch. For instance: Maybe you're vexed about a vocation audit at work. Your supervisor adulated a few things about your work. But, you're feeling down because she had one little analysis. You may even believe, "I'm nothing but bad at my specific employment." or "She doesn't care for me. I should be bad."

Concentrating on just the bad is a case of negative or contorted thinking. You can instruct yourself to look for negative thinking. You can ask yourself how obvious or accommodating your considerations were. "What did my manager state precisely?" "Were there positive remarks?" "For what reason do I center just around one criticism?"

You can figure out how to see that the harsh things you state to yourself may shield you from seeing the positive pieces of your life and work. With time and practice, you can figure out how to reveal to yourself progressively exact and supportive proclamations. You may state, "I've done a great deal of good work this year, and my manager saw it. She thought there was one zone I can improve. So I'll think about certain things I can do to get more grounded here."

CBT consolidates a few different ways to assist you in changing how you think:

- You figure out how to see irrational thoughts about yourself.

- You figure out how to stop the thoughts.

- You figure out how to supplant the negative thoughts with accurate thoughts.

- You can figure out how to loosen up your mind and body. This can bring down your stress.

- You can figure out how to deal with your time better. This can bring down your stress.

Unwanted thoughts can cause you to feel restless or discouraged. They may shield you from making an amazing most.

A technique called thought-stopping can assist you in stopping unwanted thoughts.

- What you think can influence how you feel. Thought-stopping causes you to change how you suspect as much that you feel good.

- Changing your thinking will take some time. You have to rehearse thought-stopping each day. Sooner or later, you'll have the option to stop unwanted thoughts immediately.

- A few people may require more assistance to stop unwanted thoughts. Converse with your doctor or a specialist if you need more assistance to stop thoughts that trouble you.

How can you stop your thoughts?

To stop unwanted thoughts, you center on the idea and afterward figure out how to state "Stop" to end the idea. From the start, you will yell, "Stop!" for all to hear. At that point, you will figure out how to state it in your mind so you can utilize this method anyplace. Here's how to begin:

<u>List your most stressful thoughts</u>. These are the thoughts that divert you from your day by day exercises and make you stress more. You wish you could quit having these considerations, yet they continue happening. Record your upsetting considerations arranged by the most distressing to the least unpleasant. Begin practicing thought-stopping with the idea that is the least upsetting. Here's a case of a list, beginning with the most distressing:

- I'm constantly stressed that something awful will happen to my kid, regardless of whether she just gets a cold.

- I simply realize that one of us will get laid off from work.

- I'm so apprehensive about making a presentation at work that it's all I can consider.

<u>Envision the thought</u>. Sit or rests in a private place (so you can say "Stop!" so anyone can hear and not feel hesitant). Close your eyes. Envision a circumstance where you may have this stressful thought. Permit yourself to concentrate on the idea.

<u>Stop the thought</u>. Frightening yourself is a decent method to intrude on the idea. Attempt one of these two techniques:

- Set a clock, watch, or other alarm for 3 minutes. Center

on your unwanted thought. When the clock or caution goes off, yell, "Stop!" If you need, stand up when you state, "Stop." Some individuals snap their fingers or applaud. These activities and saying "Stop" are signs of quitting thinking. Void your brain, and attempt to keep it void for around 30 seconds. If the upsetting idea returns during that time, yell, "Stop!" once more.

- Rather than utilizing a clock, you can copy yourself yelling, "Stop!" at interims of 3 minutes, 2 minutes, and 1 minute. Do the thought-stopping activity. Concentrate on the idea and afterward quit contemplating the undesirable idea—or whatever else—when you hear your recorded voice say, "Stop." Hearing your voice advising you to stop reinforces your promise to disposing of the unwanted thought.

Practice steps 1 through 3 until the idea leaves in order. Attempt the procedure once more. This time, interfere with the idea by saying, "Stop!" in a normal voice.

After your normal voice can stop the idea, take a stab at murmuring, "Stop." Over time, you can simply envision hearing "Stop" inside your mind. Now, you can stop the idea at whatever point and any place it happens.

Pick another idea that irritates you more than the last one, and proceed with thought-stopping.

Different approaches to stop thought

You can change how you do thought-stopping:

- Close your eyes and take a deep breath. Make a picture in your mind of a major, splendid red stop sign. The letters on the sign are large and white: STOP. Picture the vehicles stopping at the sign, standing by quietly until it is their chance to go. Hang tight for your turn; at that point, take a full breath and continue over the street. Is it accurate to say that you are as yet believing that unwanted thought? It will take practice, yet with time your mind will do this all alone, which will assist you in stopping unwanted thoughts.

- Make yourself aware that you have an unwanted thought by saying to yourself, "I have the idea that I may lose my job." Or "I imagine that I may lose my job." This advises you that these are thoughts, not something that will occur.

- After you stop an unwanted thought, include an increasingly charming idea or picture that causes you to feel progressively quiet. This thought and image aren't identified with the unwanted thought. For instance, you can consider playing with your children or heading out to have a great time with your companions. Or then again, you may see yourself lying on a beach.

An example of thought-stopping

Here's a case of how though stopping may work:

You're stressed over a presentation you are giving busy working later in the day. You're readied. You realize you're prepared. However, you can't quit stressing over it. You envision committing a mistake.

When you begin to consider yourself lurching over words, you state "Stop" discreetly in your brain. You get up, move around, or snap your rubber band as you state, "Stop." Then you consider something pleasant to take your mind off the thought, for example, a trip you intend to take or a movie you recently made you laugh.

Chapter 4 - What is Positive CBT? A Look at Positive Cognitive Behavioral Therapy

What rings a bell when you hear "therapy"? The vast majority have the vision of what we find in the movies, a doctor situated in his seat, with a pen and cushion close by, while the client lies down and discusses his feelings.

Although that is to be sure a sort of therapy, that doesn't give us the entire image of what therapy is and what it very well maybe.

There are numerous sorts of "therapy" in the field of Psychology. Cognitive Behavioral Therapy, all the more prevalently alluded to as CBT, is one of them. CBT has been around since the twentieth century and is known to be very successful for individuals with tension, specific behavioral issues, and even specific sorts of phobia.

If CBT is regularly utilized with explicit difficulties, what precisely is Positive CBT?

Positive Psychology has consistently evolved since it was first presented. Some portion of its development utilizes different parts of brain research and various kinds of treatment to assist individuals in prospering and flourish. CBT plays a significant role in the advancement of positive psychology as it is regularly utilized with themes like hopefulness, appreciation, and strength, among numerous others.

What is Positive Cognitive Behavioral Therapy?

Positive Cognitive Behavioral Therapy (CBT), as the name recommends, is established on the main concepts of CBT.

The CBT model was first used to assist people in explicit issues, for example, depression and anxiety. It assists people in understanding their maladaptive thoughts, which were regularly seen as the wellspring of their problems. It centers on the issue, what causes the issue, and potential mediations for the issue.

Positive CBT, then again, shifts treatment towards concentrating on what is direct with an individual and on what is working, rather than concentrating on all the issues an individual face and what isn't working.

Positive CBT and Its Relationship with Other Theories and Therapies

Positive CBT depends on a few unique theories and therapists. It draws on ideas from CBT, utilizing both Cognitive Therapy and Rational Emotive Behavior Therapy. It utilizes ideas from positive psychology, Solution-Focused Brief Therapy, and the "upward arrow" of Functional Behavior Analysis.

Cognitive Behavioral Therapy (CBT)

CBT looks to assist people in easing themselves of psychological stress through examining and amending flawed convictions, which prompts progressively fitting responses and reactions. It has been known to help with issues including discouragement, nervousness, substance use, dietary issues, and even issues seeing someone.

CBT Model

The model shows the basic premise of CBT—our thoughts, feelings, and activities influence one another. Our mental issues can somewhat be followed back to two things: faulty thinking patterns and unhelpful learned patterns of behavior.

CBT highlights the significance of looking at our thoughts, finding how these beliefs cause us to feel, and how these influence our activities. Our self-talk, or mind chatter, can give us information on what these beliefs are and if they are broken or slanted.

Positive CBT takes a look at our thoughts, emotions, and conduct. Much the same as traditional CBT, it looks to comprehend the basic musings and emotions connected to these activities. Its center isn't the place, things are broken and slanted, yet where things are working out positively. It discovers chances to make a positive move in our beliefs and thoughts with the goal that it can change how we experience life.

There are two kinds of treatments that are generally alluded to as CBT:

1. Dr. Aaron Beck's Cognitive Therapy

2. Dr. Albert Ellis' Rational Emotive Behavior Therapy.

Cognitive Therapy (CT)

During the 1960s, Dr. Beck directed investigations to test the various concept of depression ("History of Cognitive Behavior Therapy," 2019). He found that people with depression had negative thoughts, which regularly repeated. These negative thoughts frequently include oneself, the future, and the world.

This sort of CBT causes clients to challenge their dysfunctional thoughts, evaluate various potential beliefs and interpretations, and utilize those that are generally gainful to the client.

This CT model can be adjusted in Positive CBT as it looks at emotional, behavioral, and physiological responses that happen because of programmed musings and pictures. Positive CBT assists clients in recognizing positive contemplations that fuel supportive and gainful responses. In doing so, clients can intentionally decide to concentrate on these constructive thoughts, helping them reach all the more decidedly and fittingly in a specific situation.

Rational Emotive Behavior Therapy (REBT)

The goal of REBT is to enable the person to recognize the irrational belief, challenge these convictions, and change them into progressively rational ones. Dr. Ellis made the ABC Model which looks at the accompanying:

- **Enacting Event** – this is what occurs us or around us

- **Belief** – these are our understandings, recognitions, suspicions, and desires in a given circumstance

- **Consequence** – this how we feel and carry on

Our Beliefs assume a significant job by the way we wind up

feeling about a circumstance and how we decide to respond to that occasion. We frequently react without focusing on what drives us, our Beliefs, to carry on that way.

In 1987, the ABC model got known as the ABCDE model, including two additional means, Dispute, and new Effect.

Dispute intends to search for contentions and proof that will conflict with our nonsensical convictions. The new Effect is presently the result after questioning our contemplations, in this way bringing about a move in our expectations.

Positive CBT makes this ABC model a stride further and helps people react more emphatically if things turn out badly. In 2006, Martin Seligman adjusted Ellis' model and utilized ABCDE to clarify how individuals can figure out how to be increasingly hopeful.

Adversity is the occasion or circumstance that occurred. Clients are urged to incorporate subtleties of that circumstance and to be explicit and objective. It takes a gander at realities and certainties rather than understandings.

Belief is presently the musings that go through the individual's mind during the situation.

Clients are welcome to record all the things they can recollect without sifting these musings. The outcome incorporates how the client felt and how they responded during the difficulty.

Clients are approached to be explicit in depicting their feelings, responses, and activities. In the wake of recognizing the outcomes, clients are approached to look at how their results line up with their convictions and if this bodes well.

During the Disputation stage, clients are tested to produce proof to exhibit how a portion of their convictions are incorrect. They approached to look at idealistic prospects and elective convictions that are progressively precise to the given misfortune. Clients can share disputer beliefs through various ways like:

- How a belief isn't completely obvious,

- What is increasingly precise contrasted with explicitly recognized beliefs,

- Potential results for every belief,

- Progressively fitting reactions given a particular conviction,

- Also, discovering potential arrangements.

Energization moves the client's emphasis on how contesting off base beliefs changes how they feel, react, and act. Regularly, the client feels alleviation, turns out to be progressively idealistic, and can pick increasingly supportive behavior given a particular circumstance. It encourages them to concentrate on the arrangements that they had the option to concoct during disputation.

Solution Focused Brief Therapy (SFBT)

SFBT was created by Steve de Shazer and Insoo Kim Berg during the 1970s ("What is Solution-Focused Therapy," 2019). Most sorts of treatment centers around the person's concern and what occurred previously.

SFBT, centers on what's to come, is objective arranged, and tries to discover arrangements. The approach makes two suppositions; each individual comprehends what they have to improve their lives and that they have the negligible ability to make answers for themselves.

Positive CBT frequently utilizes SFBT techniques to assist people in producing arrangements and conceivable outcomes. Here are a couple of instances of SFBT techniques:

- **Previous Solutions** – The therapist poses questions about different occasions when the client had the option to take care of different issues. A potential inquiry posed is, "What worked in that issue?"

- **Present and Future-focused Questions** – Instead of posing inquiries identified with the past, the client is urged to see what is currently working. The therapist asks how the client imagines himself later on. A case of future-centered questions is, "What will you do in seven days that will tell you are gaining ground?"

- **Compliments** – These approve what the client is doing and what he is experiencing. Praises are regularly conveyed through grateful questions like "How could you do that?"

- **Accomplish more of what is working** – The therapist welcomes the client to give things a shot or to test by accomplishing a greater amount of what has worked for him previously.

- **Scaling Questions** – A size of 0 to 10 is utilized to assist clients in surveying the circumstance they are in, assess and keep tabs on their development, and discover what their next little advance can be.

Positive CBT practitioners, through SFBT techniques, help their clients roll out positive improvements by concentrating on what is in their control and what they can do, rather than what they can't do.

Functional Behavior Analysis (FBA)

A functional assessment considers conduct yet additionally

looks past the particular activity. The methodology is frequently used to comprehend why an individual demonstrations a specific way. It tries to discover factors that might be related to the conduct, just as variables that are identified when the conduct doesn't happen.

Additionally clarifies that during an FBA, an issue is examined utilizing the ABC model. The ABC factors show the probability that problematic behavior will or won't happen. The FBA procedure comprises of five steps:

- **Characterizing the Behavior** – A group recognizes the problematic behavior that should be tended to.

- **Collecting Data** – The objective of this progression is to become familiar with the conduct by taking a gander at various components identified with the conduct. The ABC model can be utilized in this step.

- **Building up a Hypothesis** – The group makes an educated guess, given the information assembled about the capacity, reasons, and motivation behind the conduct.

- **Building up an Intervention** – An intercession plan is made to help roll out fundamental improvements in the condition that will address the problematic behavior.

- **Assessing the Plan** – Once the intervention is set, the group assesses its adequacy and makes fitting changes when required.

In Positive CBT, the diverse FBA steps are regularly utilized along with the CBT and SFBT techniques. Rather than looking at problematic behavior, the FBA procedure can feature behavior that works for the client, encourages him to adapt, and can be rehashed to lead him to progress.

As talked about, the main models and ideas from CBT, SFBT, and FBA are regularly utilized in Positive CBT with a move in focus. The focal point of CBT will be talked about in the following area as it investigates the difference between traditional and Positive CBT.

Positive CBT vs. CBT: What's the Difference?

Positive CBT rose out of traditional CBT from the craving to assist clients in increasing progressively considerable and long term benefits from therapy. These two kinds of treatment have a similar goal—to achieve the ideal change in the client's life.

One noteworthy distinction between Positive CBT and its traditional predecessor is the sort of contemplations and beliefs it centers around. Customary CBT centers on problem-solving. It sees what's up and discovers potential intercessions to fix it. Frequently, it centers on the client's limitations and deficiencies.

These findings are supported by the CBT literature, which shows an accentuation on the variables that advance and continue an issue.

Then again, positive CBT centers on helping the client feel positive feelings, be locked in at home and work, have significance, experience achievements, and keep up positive relationships. It features the variables that help support the person's prosperity and permits them to thrive. It tries to help the individual look at his gifts, qualities, capacities, experience, and assets.

What will happen when we think about what is direct with individuals as opposed to focusing on what's up with them?

Positive CBT, as clarified, is grounded in a qualities based way to deal with helping individuals. This point of view underscores that the individual is competent and includes the resources inside him to manage clashes, viably adapt to unpleasant circumstances, and discover answers for his issues.

This approach supports a collaborative process between advisor and client. It urges the client to investigate his qualities and choose how he can apply these to explicit parts of his life.

Positive CBT utilizes an "upward arrow technique," which is not quite the same as traditional CBT's "downward arrow." The "downward arrow technique" encourages clients to distinguish considerations and beliefs that lead to negative emotions and practices.

It is problem-focused and frequently sees what's up. Explicit questions like "What's bad about that?" "What's not working?" "What's not helping?" and "What is the most noticeably awful thing that can occur?" are instances of downward arrow questions that are utilized in traditional CBT.

Then again, the upward arrow technique poses inquiries like, "What might you want to change?" "In what manner will you feel once that situation changes?" "Why will that matter in your life or your situations?" and "What is the ideal situation?" These emphasize the client's certain thoughts and responses. It additionally permits the client to look for prospects and find expectations for the issue.

Fredrik Bannick on Practicing Positive CBT

Practicing Positive CBT, by and large, has likenesses with traditional CBT practices. Treatment will, in general, be a collaborative effort between the therapist and the client. They cooperate to recognize maladaptive beliefs and practices that should be changed, build up a goal, and work on it.

Then again, Positive CBT places more accentuation on the

client's job in therapy. Basic components which professionals must be aware of while connecting with clients. These six components are talked about underneath:

- **Therapeutic Alliance** – The therapist and client concede to therapeutic collaborative engagement. The therapist encourages a positive association and monitors the client's advancement. The client plays a functioning job in planning his mediations and takes responsibility for the change he needs to make.

- **Build Rapport** – The positive plot begins with the therapist's questions, which are regularly equipped towards revealing the client's qualities. The questions can fill in as an icebreaker and an approach to become more acquainted with the client more.

- **Recognize Problems** – Positive CBT doesn't overlook issues. Most clients may think that it's useful to discuss their issues. Positive CBT therapists tune in to these accounts and recognize what the client is sharing. The therapist doesn't test further into the issue; rather, they center on helping the client to see the issue contrastingly and reveal qualities and potential outcomes.

- **Move to Strengths and Solutions** – The therapist asks questions to control the client to concentrate on arrangements, qualities, and accessible assets. Advisors may utilize distinctive SFBT techniques, for example, concentrating on what is working and searching for special cases to the issue.

- **Set Goals** – This is a significant component in the therapeutic process as it gives the client the chance to change. The therapist can utilize goals as an approach to move the client's concentration to conceivable outcomes, rather than issues.

- **Positive Self-Monitoring** – The client is urged to screen his advancement, qualities, and exemptions to the issue. Therapists can utilize the FBA approach to assist the client in self-monitoring. A Positive FBA approach is utilized when posing questions rather than the customary FBA. Instances of Positive FBA questions, which may appear SFBT questions, are "When things are working out positively, what have you seen that you differently?" and "If a wonder occurs, and your issues are not, at this point, your issues, what will be the first thing you notice that you are doing differently?"

Positive CBT Interventions and Techniques

As referenced before, Positive CBT depends on CBT, SFBT, and utilizations FBA. The interventions partook in this segment utilize one or a combination of these traditional intercessions. Positive CBT takes these techniques and movements them into concentrating on the person's qualities and potential arrangements, as opposed to what's going on.

The "upward arrow technique," referenced prior, is a sort of Positive CBT intercession therapist frequently use. Additionally shares a few different methods that can be utilized: changing the viewing, changing the doing, changing the inclination, schoolwork tasks, and assessment.

Change the Viewing

One of the most critical discoveries in Psychology, over the most recent 20 years, is that people can pick how they think.

As indicated by Bannick (2017), "changing the review" urges clients to change something in the manner in which they see the issue, how they do the issue or both. This mediation takes a shot at the reason that one can't anticipate various outcomes by taking part in something very similar.

This procedure centers around helping an individual change what they focus on, just as their thoughts and beliefs. Bannick shares five intercessions in this procedure:

- **Recognize Feelings and Experience** – Clients are

given the space to recognize how they feel and what they encountered previously. They are urged to investigate accommodating stories and find a kinder and progressively empathetic perspective on themselves and the situation.

- **Focus on Something Different** – Therapists manage the clients to focus on past patterns of overcoming adversity rather than issues and disappointments. This enables the client to move how they see themselves, which can bring about a progressively positive view of oneself.

- **Concentrate on What Clients Want for the Future** – Instead of concentrating on what they don't care for in their current circumstance or the past, specialists help their clients center around what they need later on. Clients set objectives and spotlight on what they need to change. This encourages them to see the potential outcomes as opposed to focusing on the issues.

- **Challenge Unhelpful Beliefs** – Therapists utilize Positive CBT to control clients to discover accommodating thoughts and adaptive behavior that can build their positive encounters of themselves and the world. The procedure causes them to discover thoughts and practices that the client, as of now, employments. Accentuation is set on rehashing this adaptive cognition and activities.

- **Utilize a Spiritual Perspective** – Three Cs of spirituality: association, sympathy, and commitment. Specialists welcome clients to investigate interfacing with something greater past themselves. The client finds ways to be progressively compassionate or kinder towards himself as well as other people. Finally, the clients are urged to contribute and unselfishly be of service to other people. These three Cs have been discovered the source of resilience.

Change the Doing

Positive CBT considers the example of behavior and discovers approaches to break that design. Rather than searching for reasons why the difficulty exists, clients survey what they are doing to take care of their problem.

The primary intervention used to "change the doing" is to focus on patterns of conduct. These patterns can be things that occur all alone or include others as well. They are welcome to change a piece of their practiced activities through two specific techniques:

Paradox – Therapists welcome the client to investigate the issue and to discover approaches to heighten it or to get it going all the more frequently. The client attempts to get it going purposely. This permits the client to acknowledge that there is an issue, and perhaps let it play out.

Link New Actions – Clients distinguish something they can do when the issue happens. Another conduct is acquainted with break the problematic pattern. This new activity is preferably something that will end up being beneficial for them, which might be a challenge as well.

The subsequent intervention is to focus on the practices the client participates in when things are working out in a good way. This gives the client the space to find exceptions cases in the issue, times when the problematic behavioral pattern was absent.

When the client discovers this exception, the client is welcome to investigate what they were doing at that point, what was going on during that time, and what discloses to them that the difficult behavior has finished or is going to end. The client is urged to take part in these supportive activities purposefully, similarly as they did during the occasions when the issue was absent.

To change the doing, clients must discover approaches to accomplish something unexpectedly. Regularly, problematic behavior continues as an issue because the client does things again and again.

Through Positive CBT, therapists believe that the solutions are as of now accessible to the clients, that clients are the best individuals to comprehend what works and what doesn't, and that clients can cause changes in the manner they carry because that they have just made changes previously.

Change the Feeling

When the questions in therapy focus on the problem, negative influence diminishes, however, doesn't build a positive effect. Then again, questions that focus on conceivable outcomes and solutions help decrease negative effects yet additionally increment positive effect. People increase better comprehension of their issues.

Positive CBT centers around positive feelings by utilizing addresses identified with trust, achievement, qualities, and skills; the broaden-and-build theory proposes that positive feelings permit people to expand their awareness of their convictions and practices.

A focus on positive feelings supports new thoughts and activities. Therapists ask open-ended questions that focus on what the client needs, just as on what is now working and what can support the client.

Through utilizing CBT, SFBT, and FBA, and applying these

techniques with regards to Positive CBT, therapists can assist clients in concentrating on the aptitudes and resources accessible to them.

Homework

Positive CBT, just as traditional CBT, utilizes schoolwork to drive change, particularly since change regularly occurs between therapy sessions. In treatment, the client learns new standards. After therapy, the client would now be able to follow up on this new learning and practice specific interventions that were investigated during the session.

Traditional CBT utilizes behavioral experiments. Positive CBT utilizes these behavioral experiments, once more, concentrating on what is right and working. Here are a couple of instances of behavioral tests and how they are utilized in Positive CBT:

Experimental manipulation of the environment – The client is to have a go at something new, something else from what he typically does in a particular setting. Like previous techniques, the client explores by finding exceptions to the issue, purposefully attempting these activities that added to that exemption.

Observational experiments – The client assembles

information and searches for evidence that underpins their beliefs. For this situation, clients are approached to discover evidence for their positive thoughts, rather than their negative beliefs. These experiments help clients through attention bias, which expands our chances to see positive confirmation when we focus on our positive thoughts.

Discovery-orientation experiments – The client is welcome to collect data by investigating what can occur if he occupied with a particular behavior. The client may evaluate the conduct to acquire the necessary information. One method of utilizing a discovery-oriented experiment is by welcoming the client to imagine that they are now, later on, needed for themselves. At that point, the client investigates what he is doing in that future, what is unique, how they are feeling and acting, and even what their relationships resemble in that future.

Note that homework is given if the client consents to it and sees the incentive in it. Homework will have a more likely effect if the client recognizes how they can benefit by doing such homework.

5 Positive CBT Exercises

Up until this point, we examined Positive CBT with regards to therapy and how clients experience these in a meeting. There are numerous different ways Positive CBT can be utilized. Huge numbers of positive brain psychology-based activities and intercessions utilize the ideas of Positive CBT. There are a few activities that are accessible in the Positive Psychology Toolkit.

Here is a couple of you can take a stab at your own. You can look at the toolkit for the full subtleties of each activity and find significantly more activities you can benefit by.

1. Daily Exceptions Journal

Goal: To expand awareness about their strengths and capacities.

Activity: Answer the accompanying questions:

- When didn't I experience the problem today?

- What improved today, even just a little bit?

- What did I do another way to improve things?

- What would I be able to do to proceed with these improvements?

- What will my life resemble if these improvements proceed?

2. Strengths Spotting by Exception Finding

Goal: To produce expectations and increase self-efficacy.

Activity: Answer the accompanying questions as most ideal as while thinking about a particular problem/concern in mind.

Finding Exceptions:

- Was there when this problem was not a problem?

- How was it during that time?

- What were you doing rather during that time?

Searching for Solutions:

- When confronted with an overwhelming challenge, what is your "go-to" way to conquer it?

- What was the best project you take a shot at? What made you successful?

Concentrating on Strengths:

Which of your strengths did you use to manage your present issue or overcome problems before? Recognize at least 5.

How might you utilize these strengths to gain ground towards your desired goal?

How might you utilize these strengths to adapt to future

challenges?

3. Three Good Things

Goal: To practice appreciation and move what and how we focus on things.

Activity:

- Record three beneficial things about your day.

- Consider how you added to causing these things to occur.

4. Benefit Finding

Goal: To boost resilience and make awareness that difficult life events may have benefits.

Activity: Write down a previous challenge or issue you had. One that has just been settled or is presently not, at this point, challenge. Answer the accompanying questions:

- How did that challenge change you?

- What did you gain from that experience?

- How did that experience help you grow as an individual?

5. You, At Your Best

Goal: To recognize and use their strengths and increment positive emotions through relishing when they were at their best.

Activity: Think of a story when you were at your best. This was likely a second when you had the option to beat a test, improve a positive experience, felt pleased with yourself, and felt glad to be alive.

- Record your story. Be as explicit and precise as could reasonably be expected. Remember the accompanying things for your story:
    - The events or details in what you were encountering.
    - The job you played in that circumstance.
    - What you did that contributed or helped the circumstance.
    - What you did that you had the option to profit by or others profited by.
    - Your emotions and feelings during that experience.
- Ensure your story has a beginning, middle, and end.

- Read your story. As you read, feature the words or phrases that you consider as strengths.

- Make a list of the things you featured. Consider this and perceive how you do these at present.

A Take-Home Message

Positive CBT utilizes similar procedures and models of traditional CBT. It additionally utilizes techniques and intercessions from SFBT and FBA. The Positive CBT process causes people to concentrate on what works and what is directly about them and the circumstance they are in. However, it utilizes techniques and activities that are utilized in different kinds of therapies, continually concentrating on the positive.

Mediations utilizing Positive CBT have helped clients with appreciation, hopefulness, mentality, and strength.

You can't return and change the start; however, you can begin where you are and change the ending.

While looking at the past and assessing our issues is useful, Positive CBT promotes that more drawn out enduring advantages are achieved by concentrating on what we can change, which is our present and future. We can accomplish these progressions by focusing on our accommodating thoughts and beliefs, just as our adaptive behaviors.

When we have recognized our capacities, resources, and qualities, Positive CBT urges us to accomplish a greater amount of these and make small shifts in the way we get things done to accomplish the future we need for ourselves.

Chapter 5 - Cognitive-Behavioral Therapy for Depression and Anxiety

There is a wide range of ways to deal with psychotherapy. A few therapists relate to a specific methodology or direction, while others draw from a wide range of approaches. Cognitive-behavioral therapy (CBT) is one explicit direction of psychotherapy that looks to assist individuals in changing how they think.

Cognitive Behavioral Therapy

Cognitive-behavioral therapy depended on cognitive theory and was created by Aaron Beck for anxiety and depression. CBT is a mix of cognitive and behavioral therapies that help patients tune into their internal dialogue to change maladaptive thinking patterns. Beck created explicit methods to help challenge a depressive client's assumptions and convictions and assist patients in figuring out how to change their deduction to be increasingly practical and hence lead to feeling much improved. There is additionally an accentuation on problem-solving and changing practices, and clients are urged to play a functioning job in their therapy.

Different Types of Cognitive-Behavioral Therapy

One kind of CBT is rational emotive behavioral therapy (REBT), which was created by Albert Ellis. Ellis thinks about strong feelings to result from a collaboration between events in nature and our convictions and beliefs. A portion of these beliefs can be excessively strong or unbending. For instance, you are keeping up the belief that everybody should like you. With REBT, you would figure out how to change that belief, so it is less extraordinary and more reluctant to meddle with your life. Your belief could then change to needing individuals to like you yet understanding that not every person will.

Another type of CBT is dialectical behavioral therapy (DBT), which was created by Marsha Linehan principally to be utilized for patients with borderline personality disorder (BPD). DBT stresses taking a shot at tolerating thoughts and emotions as opposed to attempting to fight them. The objective is to get patients to acknowledge their thoughts and emotions with the goal that they can, in the long run, change them.

Exposure and response prevention therapy (ERP) is one more

CBT that is normally utilized for the obsessive-compulsive disorder (OCD). In this therapy, patients are presented to the circumstances or objects that cause them the most fear (fixations); however, they can't take part in the practices that help soothe the anxiety they feel (impulses). For instance, if you fear germs, during ERP, your therapist may have you touch money and afterward not wash your hands for a particular measure of time. Practicing this, again and again, causes you to gain trust in managing the going with anxiety and can extraordinarily help ease the side effects of OCD with repeated exposure.

Does CBT Work for Depression?

It has been hard to look into the adequacy of psychotherapy since the term can allude to such huge numbers of various exercises. Intellectual conduct treatment, be that as it may, loans itself well to look into and has been experimentally demonstrated to be successful in treating side effects of depression and anxiety. It will, in general, be a short-to direct term, rather than some different directions on account of its attention on the present, just as on critical thinking. Its strategic instruct the patient to figure out how to turn into their advisor makes it a drawn-out treatment.

Medications or Psychotherapy?

Depression and anxiety can be treated with prescriptions, psychotherapy, or both. Some exploration has demonstrated that the combination of medication and treatment can be especially compelling.

Insurance companies sometimes there urge family doctors to recommend meds as opposed to alluding to a mental health professional for psychotherapy. There are times when this might be suitable, yet there are different occasions when psychotherapy is shown. If you are taking an upper or a tension medicine and you accept that the issue isn't being tended to, think about looking for help from a mental health professional.

Therapy for Anxiety Disorders

Regardless of whether you're suffering from panic attacks, over the top worries, tenacious concerns, or debilitating fear, realize that you don't need to live with anxiety and fear. Treatment can help, and for some anxiety problems, treatment is regularly the best option. That is because anxiety therapy—in contrast to anxiety medication—treats something other than the side effects of the issue. Therapy can assist you in revealing the fundamental reasons for your concerns and fears; figure out how to unwind; look at circumstances in new, less startling ways; and grow better adapting and problem-solving skills. Therapy gives you the tools to overcome anxiety and shows you how to utilize them.

Anxiety disorders contrast impressively, so therapy ought to be tailored to your particular symptoms and diagnosis. If you have obsessive-compulsive disorder (OCD), for instance, your treatment will be unique about somebody who needs assistance for anxiety attacks. The length of therapy will rely upon the sort and seriousness of your anxiety disorder. But, numerous anxiety therapies are generally short-term. As indicated by the American Psychological Association, numerous individuals improve fundamentally inside 8 to 10 therapy sessions.

While a wide range of therapy is utilized to treat anxiety, the main methodologies are cognitive behavioral therapy (CBT) and exposure therapy. Every anxiety therapy might be utilized alone or joined with different sorts of therapy. Anxiety therapy might be led independently, or it might occur in a group of individuals with similar anxiety problems. In any case, the goal is the equivalent: to bring down your anxiety levels, calm your mind, and overcome your fears.

Cognitive-behavioral therapy (CBT) for anxiety

Cognitive-behavioral therapy (CBT) is the most broadly utilized therapy for anxiety disorder. Research has demonstrated it to be compelling in the treatment of panic disorder, phobias, social anxiety disorder, and generalized anxiety disorder among numerous different conditions.

CBT addresses negative patterns and distortions in the way we look at the world and ourselves. As the name proposes, this includes two main components:

Cognitive therapy analyzes how negative thoughts, or cognitions, add to nervousness.

Behavior therapy looks at how you act and respond in circumstances that trigger anxiety.

The essential reason of CBT is that our thoughts—not outside occasions—influence how we feel. It's not the circumstance you're in that decides how you feel; however, your impression of the circumstance. For instance, envision that you've quite recently been welcome to a big party. Think about three distinct perspectives regarding the invitation, and how those contemplations would influence your feelings.

As should be obvious, a similar event can prompt various feelings in various individuals. Everything relies upon our desires, mentalities, and convictions. For individuals with anxiety disorders, negative perspectives fuel the negative feelings of nervousness and fear. The goal of cognitive-behavioral therapy for anxiety is to distinguish and address these negative thoughts and beliefs. The thought is if you change how you want to change how you feel.

Thought to challenge in CBT for anxiety

Thought challenging—otherwise called cognitive restructuring—is a procedure wherein you challenge the negative thinking patterns that add to your anxiety, supplanting them with increasingly positive, realistic thoughts. This includes three steps:

- **Recognizing your negative thoughts**. With anxiety disorders, circumstances are seen as more dangerous than they truly seem to be. To somebody with a germ phobia, for instance, shaking someone else's hand can appear dangerous. Although you may handily observe this is an irrational fear, recognizing your own silly, alarming thoughts can be troublesome. One strategy is to ask yourself what you were thinking when you began feeling anxious. Your therapist will assist you in this progression.

- **You are testing your negative thoughts**. In the subsequent step, your therapist will show you how to assess your anxiety-provoking thoughts. This includes scrutinizing the evidence for your frightening thoughts, investigating unhelpful convictions, and testing out the truth of negative expectations. Strategies for testing negative considerations incorporate leading investigations, gauging the advantages and disadvantages of stressing or avoiding the thing you fear, and deciding the practical possibilities that what you're anxious about will occur.

- **You were supplanting negative thoughts with realistic thoughts**. When you've recognized the irrational predictions and negative distortions in your anxious thoughts, you can supplant them with new considerations that are increasingly exact and positive. Your therapist may assist you in concocting reasonable, quieting explanations you can say to yourself when you're confronting or foreseeing a circumstance that regularly sends your anxiety levels taking off.

Exposure therapy for anxiety

Anxiety is not a wonderful sensation, so it's just normal to evade it if you can. One of the manners in which individuals do this is by avoiding the circumstances that make them anxious. If you have a fear of heights, you may drive three hours out of your approach to abstain from crossing a tall bridge. Or on the other hand, if the possibility of open talking leaves your stomach in knots, you may skirt your best friend's wedding to abstain from giving a toast. Besides the inconvenience factor, the issue with avoiding your feelings of trepidation is that you never get the opportunity to defeat them. Avoid your feelings of fear regularly makes them more grounded.

Exposure therapy, as the name proposes, opens you to the situations or objects you fear. The idea is that through rehashed exposures, you'll feel an expanding feeling of command over the circumstance, and your anxiety will reduce. The exposure is done in one of two different ways: Your therapist may request that you envision the frightening circumstance, or you may stand up to it in real life. Exposure therapy might be utilized alone, or it might be led as a feature of cognitive-behavioral therapy.

Systematic desensitization

Instead of confronting your biggest fear immediately, which can be damaging, exposure therapy typically begins with a circumstance that is just somewhat undermining and works up from that point. This step-by-step approach is called systematic desensitization. Systematic desensitization permits you to progressively challenge your feelings of fear, form certainty, and master skills for controlling panic.

Facing the fear of flying

Step 1: Look at photographs of planes.

Step 2: Watch a video of a plane in flight.

Step 3: Watch real planes take off.

Step 4: Book a plane ticket

Step 5: Pack for your flight.

Step 6: Drive to the airport.

Step 7: Check-in for your flight.

Step 8: Wait for boarding.

Step 9: Get on the plane.

Step 10: Take the flight.

Systematic desensitization includes three parts:

You were learning relaxation skills. In the first place, your therapist will show you relaxation techniques, for example, progressive muscle relaxation or deep breathing. You'll practice in treatment and all alone at home. When you begin going up against your apprehensions, you'll utilize this relaxation technique to diminish your physical anxiety response (for example, trembling and hyperventilating) and empower relaxation.

You are creating a step-by-step list. Next, you'll make a list of 10 to 20 scary circumstances that progress toward your final objective. For instance, if your final objective is to beat your fear of flying, you may begin by looking at photographs of planes and end with taking a real flight. Each progression ought to be as explicit as reasonably expected, with a clear, measurable objective.

You were working through the steps. Under the direction of your therapist, you'll start to work through the list. The objective is to remain in each alarming circumstance until your feelings of fear die down. That way, you'll discover that the sentiments won't hurt you, and they do leave. Each time the anxiety gets excessively extreme, you will change to the relaxation technique you learned. When you're loose once more, you can turn your consideration back to the circumstance. In this way, you will work through the means until you're ready to finish every one without feeling excessively bothered.

Complementary therapies for anxiety disorder

As you investigate your anxiety disorder in therapy, you may need to explore different avenues regarding complementary therapies intended to bring your general feelings of anxiety down and assist you in accomplishing emotional balance.

Exercise is a natural stress buster and anxiety reliever. Research shows that as meager as 30 minutes of activity three to five times each week can give significant anxiety relief. To accomplish the greatest benefit, focus on if an hour of aerobic exercise on most days.

Relaxation techniques, for example, mindfulness meditation and progressive muscle relaxation, when rehearsed routinely, can diminish tension and increment sentiments of emotional well-being.

Biofeedback utilizes sensors that measure specific physiological functions, for example, pulse, breathing, and muscle pressure—to instruct you to perceive your body's anxiety response and figure out how to control it utilizing relaxation techniques.

Hypnosis is once in a while utilized in mix with CBT for anxiety. While you're in a condition of profound unwinding, the trance inducer utilizes diverse remedial strategies to assist you in confronting your feelings of trepidation and taking a gander at them in new ways.

Making anxiety therapy work for you

There is no quick fix for anxiety. Defeating an anxiety disorder requires significant investment and commitment. Therapy includes confronting your apprehensions as opposed to avoiding them, so some of the time, you'll feel more regrettable before you improve. The significant thing is to stay with treatment and follow your therapist's recommendation. In case you're feeling debilitated with the pace of recovery, recollect that therapy of anxiety is exceptionally viable over the long run. You'll receive the rewards if you oversee it.

You can support your anxiety therapy by settling on positive decisions. Everything from your activity level to your public activity influences anxiety. Set up for progress by settling on a conscious decision to promote, imperativeness, and a positive mental viewpoint in your regular daily existence.

Learn about anxiety. To conquer anxiety, it's essential to comprehend the issue. That is the place instruction comes in. Training alone won't fix an anxiety disorder; however, it will assist you in taking advantage of therapy.

Develop your associations with others. Loneliness and isolation set up for anxiety. You are lessening your weakness by connecting with others. Make it a point to see companions; join a self-improvement or care group; share your concerns and worries with a confided in adored one.

Adopt a healthy way of life propensities. Physical activity calms pressure and uneasiness, so set aside a few minutes for regular exercise. Try not to utilize alcohol and medications to adapt to your indications, and attempt to stay away from energizers, for example, caffeine and nicotine, which can aggravate anxiety worse.

Diminish stress in your life. Analyze your life for stress, and search for approaches to limit it. Stay away from individuals who make you restless, disapprove of additional obligations, and set aside a few minutes for the sake of entertainment and relaxation in your day by day plan.

Chapter 6 - How CBT to help in boosting mindfulness, resilience, assertiveness, and self-esteem

What is Mindfulness Therapy? (Definition)

Meditation is an old-fashioned type of contemplative practice that was created as a significant part of the world's extraordinary spiritual traditions. From mindfulness meditation to creative visualization, the various types of meditation that have created all through the world all have the objective of creating and upgrading serenity, empathy, and intelligence. Recently has present-day science started to perceive the positive effects of meditation on the mind, including expanded feeling guidelines, reduced psychological distress, improved attention, and improved immune framework working? Therefore, individuals who are not associated with a spiritual tradition have started to profit by this ancient practice as a method of improving quality of life. Coming up next is a concise introduction to a particular type of meditation called mindfulness.

The reason for mindfulness meditation is to bring your mind completely into the current second, without being occupied by unrelated thoughts, or unhelpful decisions. We are normally up to speed in our thoughts, not understanding we are completely detached from what we are doing. This can have many negative outcomes, the most significant being we pass up completely engaging in our lives, with our brain on autopilot. New research has shown that when we are up to speed in our thoughts, our state of mind takes a significant dip. Alternately, when our find is focused around the current second, our mind-set is normally improved, in any event, when we might be doing something unpleasant.

Mindfulness, from a therapeutic, secular point of view, is a conscious awareness with our current second. This incorporates openness and non-judgment about the experience. It is regularly combined with different kinds of treatment, for example, Cognitive-based Therapy (CBT), Dialectical Behavior Therapy (DBT), or Acceptance and Commitment Therapy (ACT).

Mindfulness therapy isn't worried about relaxation, though that may be a result of certain practices. The focus is on expanding our consciousness of the thoughts, feelings, and actions that impede our advancement. When we are better ready to do that, we can connect with those parts of ourselves, figure out how to change our language, and pick how to react.

There are numerous approaches to practice mindfulness. The following are a few distractions for developing a simple daily meditation practice of being aware of the breath.

Locate a calm spot free of distractions. Your psyche will offer enough distractions of its own, so a spot where there is a commotion or a great deal of action will make supported consideration fundamentally more difficult.

Take a load off and close your eyes. There is no correct method to sit. You can sit with cross legs, full lotus, or upstanding in a seat. The most significant thing is that your sitting position is agreeable and not distracting itself.

Carry your psyche to the impression of your breath entering and leaving your nose. Simply notice the shivering as cool air enters and warm air exits. This is a simple task in that there are not many steps or complex visualizations to keep track of. However, you will discover it is a difficult task. You will see your mind wandering to a wide range of things: physical sensations, arranging, fantasizing, and repeating past occasions. That will be normal. The better you become at care, the more you notice how occupied you become when trying to focus your mind.

All you need to do when you notice your brain leaving your breath is tenderly bring it back. Over and over. If your mind wanders 100 times in a single moment, get it back multiple times one moment. Once in a while, people become debilitated because their minds continually wander. As a general rule, you ought to congratulate yourself for seeing your mind drifting. This is a noteworthy improvement over never seeing.

Watch your relaxing for around 5 minutes. Persistently mindful of when your mind leaves. You are continually bringing it back. After that, you may see an expanded feeling of quiet that you can use to establish the pace for the rest of the day.

As you become more familiar with the training, you can expand the time sitting to 10, 15, 20 minutes. The most significant purpose of building up a day by day reflection practice is consistency, so 3 minutes consistently is better than an hour once every week.

Try this simple practice for yourself and see what you notice. You may simply see that accepting a couple of moments as a present is rewarding enough that you search for different opportunities for the day to be available. Similarly, as this training is focused around the breath, you carefully center on driving, eating, drinking your morning mug of coffee, and visiting with a colleague. There are unlimited opportunities to associate with the current second.

Research and Studies on its Effectiveness

Most researches base on two specific types of care preparing.

The first is mindfulness-based stress reduction (MBSR) pioneered by Jon Kabat-Zinn. The second is mindfulness-based cognitive therapy (MBCT). John Teasdale, Zindek Segal, and Mark Williams—all advisors—made MBCT.

MBCT began from cognitive therapy, and it incorporates methods, for example, care reflection, yoga, and other inward-focused activities.

Treatments utilizing care have the name mindfulness-based interventions or MBIs. The exploration outlined below tried to decide the effectiveness of different kinds; but, MBSR and MBCT still get the most consideration. What follows in this area, and later in this article, are a few results you can, or can't, anticipate from using some type of MBIs.

Kuyken and partners (2015) asserted that MBCT is a viable and savvy technique for treating and preventing relapse in depressive patients. In their randomly controlled investigation, they looked at two groups: the principal got maintenance antidepressants, and the second MBCT-TS (tightened support). The trial proceeded for two years.

Sometimes research findings don't support the speculation. That was the situation for Kuyken and his fellow researchers. They found that "cost-effectiveness investigation doesn't support the hypothesis that MBCT-TS is more practical than maintenance antidepressants, as far as either relapse or recurrence." They did, however, express that the two medicines give positive results that last. Since this is the situation, they suggested they proceeded with study, and that MBCT could be helpful for high-risk patients.

Good mindfulness-awareness practices (MAP) projects can decrease apparent worry in urban communities. Analysts actualized the Mindful Awareness Practices for Daily Living 1 for 127 residents (for the most part, Caucasian and female). Their discoveries support that MAPs offer "a promising methodology for overall public health promotion." The UCLA MAPs program, which was their model, includes the following:

- Overview of Mindfulness

- Mindfulness of the Body

- Obstacles to Mindfulness

- Mindfulness to help with Physical Pain

- Working with Difficult Emotions

- Cultivating Positive Emotions

- Working with Difficult Thoughts

- Mindful Interactions

Students also get familiar with a variety of practices. Some are:

- Sitting meditation

- Standing meditation

- Practices to create positive feelings; and,

- Relational care

In 2017, Hofmann and Gomez also read MBIs for tension and sadness. They stated that MBIs have "reliably outperform [ed] non-confirm based medicines and dynamic control conditions." Their instances of these are health education, relaxation training, and psychotherapy.

Inquiring about the effectiveness of MBIs isn't without its difficulties. Some regular issues are that a few investigations do include a control group or have too hardly any members. They also here and there need to lack diversity, just like the case in the study. The most reliable research supporting MBIs originates from studies, including MBSR or MBCT.

6 Mindfulness Therapy Techniques

During mindfulness meditation, expert practitioner aides an individual or people to concentrate on the current second. This isn't generally a simple undertaking. Frequently, our brain wanders. To battle this, the expert trains members to acknowledge the wandering brain without judgment. She also may advise the individual to see where their psyche went before reeling it back to the present.

In the case of practicing alone, you should seriously think about utilizing some clock. Meditation need not belong. If you are a beginner, make progress toward one moment. This thought of beginning little, supported by exploring done by BJ Fogg, reduce barriers to beginning another habit.

Body scanning and walking also are choices or options in contrast to more traditional types of meditation. Thich Nhat Hanh clarifies the objective of walking meditation is to be the "happiest person in the world." If you can do this, you are effective. There is no goal as a primary concern. "Walking is an end in itself."

Guided imagery additionally is a well-known type of mindfulness. Some call this creative visualization or perception. In any case, the training includes inferring, through pictures, the words one hears. There are a variety of ways to practice this with and without a specialist. Shakti Gawain's book, Creative Visualization, is a nice jumping-off point if you might want to investigate this subject all alone. Don't hesitate to leave your proposals in the remarks for instruments you use or books you've found useful.

Breathing methods are a great method to pick up control when you feel on edge or focused. For instance, you can practice belly breathing—spot one hand on your stomach and the other on your chest. Breathe in, filling your tummy with air, pushing your hand out.

Allow your breath to fill your lungs, pushing your other hand out. At last, gradually breathe out. You also could choose to hold the inhalation for a specified check.

A huge number of individuals practice yoga, and all things considered. In addition to the fact that it increases your flexibility, but it also helps decreases pressure and focuses your mind. Scientist Catherine Woodyard (2011) found that also these advantages, helpful yoga:

- Enhances muscle quality,

- Improves respiratory and cardiovascular capacity,

- Helps individuals recoup from addictions,

- Reduces tension, depression, and chronic pain; and,

- Improves rest.

Is it true that you are keen on finding out additional? Sitting Together: Essential Skills for Mindfulness-Based Psychotherapy may be helpful to you. You will find why care, in a therapeutic setting, is valuable to the client and therapist. They also share how to start implementing it.

Different Types of Therapy That Incorporate Mindfulness

Dialectical Behavior Therapy (DBT) helps the individual in identifying and changing damaging thinking patterns. It includes working with a trained therapist to figure out how to apply DBT skills. Clients also can work in group settings, which allows them a chance to practice newly acquired skills.

Two other delivery modes are in-the-second telephone instructing and meeting groups for therapists. Initially created to treat borderline character issues, it also is powerful in rewarding PTSD, self-harm, and suicidal thoughts.

DBT unites together opposites. For instance, clients figure out how to replace black or white intuition with "and" thinking. DBT is tied in with offsetting acknowledgment with change. It remembers a focus on mindfulness, relational viability, trouble resistance, and emotion regulation. The vast majority of us know about the initial two, so how about we investigate the keep going ones on this list.

Distress tolerance teaches a client how to acknowledge feelings as they seem to be, at the time. There is no compelling reason to get some distance from the feeling to a limited extent since one probably won't have the option to roll out a quick improvement. Therefore, an acknowledgment that is non-evaluative and non-critical gets significant. Acceptance doesn't mean we approve of whatever is going on. It only methods we acknowledge it for what it is at that time.

Emotional regulation is, to some degree, about recognizing and labeling our emotions. This isn't in every case simple, especially if the client has needed to suppress this previously or was just ready to express extremes. There are nuances to emotional expression that DBT permits clients to learn and practice. Clients additionally figure out how to manage obstructions to evolving feelings.

Acknowledgment and Commitment Therapy additionally incorporates care. This evidenced-based approach is tied in with being available to what pesters us and effectively picking a game-plan. Mindfulness practices help clients with doing this and form the bridge between acceptance and commitment.

An establishment for ACT is the Relational Frame Theory. This thinks about the language and learning we take part in through social systems. The networks we develop show all over the place and in all things. Ignoring them is virtually impossible. Social taking in originates from behavioral learning. It is the 'why' behind the acknowledgment part of ACT. In the act of ACT, we are observers.

ACT is ground-breaking since it places you in charge of your "thoughts, feelings, sensations, and memories" (Gordon, 2018). Care (awareness) turns into a tool that helps us see those things more clearly.

A Look at using it in a Group Context

A preferred critical position of offering bunch treatment is the decrease in cost to the client. The worry that wet blankets up is whether group therapy is better than, on a par with, or more awful than singular treatment. In 2015, Sundquist and partners set up an 8-week randomized controlled study to find out.

Their findings surprised even them. Contrasts between the gathering and individual settings were not critical. They concluded that group therapy was "non-sub-par compared to treatment as normal for patients with depressive, anxiety, or stress and adjustment disorders."

Probably the best case of MBIs utilized in a gathering setting is the MBSR program. Created and implemented by Jon Kabat-Zinn, this deep-dive into common care is as intense as it is empowering. The other prove based model is MBCT. Mediations as retreats, online, and cell phone application petitions, just as brief mediations, have helpful impacts.

Mindfulness Therapy for Couples

The nuts and bolts of care at the individual level works for couples, as well. Some may contend that start with oneself is the best spot to begin. That could be valid. On the other side, something is uplifting about learning care with your partner.

Rather than, or possibly in addition to, practicing with outsiders, you get the advantage of working with somebody you know and who knows you. You also get the gift of seeing each other heal and grow. This can increment and set the bond you share.

Couples gain proficiency with the Four Foundations of Mindfulness. They are care of your body, feelings, brain, or consciousness, and how your mind works.

How would you do this? Utilizing a portion of similar activities, you would if you were doing it all alone–body scan, mindfulness meditation, and breathe work. These three are especially useful in getting you in contact with your feelings, sensations, and perceptions in the present moment.

They also help you to move in the direction of awkward feelings and acknowledge them. As a couple, you have a chance to gain empathy and understanding for one another.

Care Therapy and Depression

MBCT, DBT, and ACT are all helpful in rewarding different degrees of depression. Every join care with observing, dissecting, accepting, and choosing alternative behaviors. Clinicians realize that emotional regulation is hard for depressed patients. This is one of the qualities of DBT. It expressly centers on building this skill. But what if the patient's reactions could turn out to be more adaptive. This is the thing that Berking and partners (2019) needed to test.

They utilized an affect regulation training (ART) mediation and looked at it against a waitlist control condition (WLC) and a condition for controlling regular factors.

Craft members got guidance on,

- Muscle relaxation,

- Breathing relaxation,

- Non-critical perception and depiction of one's feelings,

- Acceptance and resilience of undesired feelings,

- Compassionate self-support when attempting to adapt to such emotions,

- Constructive investigation of the antecedents and results of one's emotions; and,

- Active change of one's emotions toward an ideal bearing.

Individuals in the treatment bunch learned and practiced specific skill-building exercises. They made and followed their daily training schedule, approached CDs to direct ability securing, and could get writings with short workouts included one 180-minute session per week for six consecutive weeks. After included one 180-minute meeting every week for six continuous weeks, members went through an additional month rehearsing for the most part, all alone. An hour and a half promoter occurred in week eight. Preparing happened in gatherings of four to eight individuals.

Their results showed that compared with the shortlist gathering, support in the ART bunch "was related with a greater reduction decrease of depressive symptom severity." The difference between ART and CFC was not statistically significant.

In light of their findings, we presently have a better understanding of the job improving feeling guideline can play in the treatment of depression.

Utilizing Mindfulness Therapy to Treat Anxiety

Do many studies contend that care can reduce anxiety, but is this reality or fiction? Hofmann, Sawyer, Witt, and Oh (2010) evaluated thirty-nine examinations and found that care based treatment essentially improved anxiety.

Individuals experiencing gentle to more extreme anxiety also experience raised feelings of anxiety. Goyal and associates (2015) explored the value of care reflection for decreasing pressure. Their survey included 47 trials with more than 3000 members. They found:

• Moderate proof of improved anxiety and depression at about two months; however

• Low proof of improved pressure/trouble

• Low proof for emotional health-related quality of life

• Low proof of no impact or inadequate evidence of any impact of reflection programs on, positive state of mind, thoughts, substance use, dietary patterns, sleep, or weight

• No proof that reflection programs were superior to any active treatment.

That appears somewhat contradictory, but the analysts do bolster the potential handiness of reflection programs. They also stress the requirement for more grounded examination designs in the future.

Will Mindfulness-Based Therapy Help Treat Insomnia?

Do you experience difficulty resting? Do you wake during the night and think that it's hard to come back to rest? Utilizing mindfulness meditation, Black and associates (2015) set out to enable older adults to improve their rest. Members had moderate sleep disturbances. Two groups were either allotted to a sleep hygiene education (SHE) or MAPs intercession. The randomized controlled trial proceeded for one year.

The MAPs intercession improved rest quality at "quick post-meditation, which was better than an exceptionally organized SHE intervention." This is incredible news for any individual who needs better quality shuteye. The impacts of poor sleep impair cognition, increase one's waistline, and feeling of anxiety.

3 Mindfulness Therapy Exercises and Games

Scour the Internet, and you will discover plenty of care games and activities. There are some for grown-ups, children, pre-teenagers, and kids. As opposed to giving you a laundry list of sites to review, here are three activities with three different objectives.

1. Givens

The essential thought of this activity, acquired from Mindfulness, Acceptance, and Positive Psychology, is disarmingly simple. In light of a statement from the US Declaration of Independence, "We hold these realities to act naturally obvious," clients investigate their life suppositions.

They also evaluate things they accept and never need to address, or those thoughts that they consider to be self-evident, i.e., guaranteed. In a clinical setting, this is schoolwork, and clients have seven days to finish it.

After restoring, the specialist drives a discussion about the person's assumptions. What themes surface? What are the client's fundamental assumptions about their life or conditions? Does the therapist need to move a few assumptions to enable the client to move forward?

2. Getting it done with Gratitude

For this activity, taken from Activities for Teaching Positive Psychology, members will review a difficult memory. The therapist gives clients early notification with the goal that they have the opportunity to consider the memory they need to share. At that point, clients get guidelines to write on it, such that helps them thankfully reappraise the memory.

Thankful individuals will, in general arrangement, well with difficult circumstances. When completed, clients check their feeling of conclusion and the emotional impact of the memory. This action incorporates suggested language and worksheets available in the book.

3. Utilizing a Strengths Approach to Build Perspective-Taking Capacity

This small-group activity assists clients in bettering to understand strengths in themselves as well as other people. The backdrop for this is the VIA Character Strength stock or the Clifton Strengths Finder. Separation of the group into small groups to examine a particular quality and how to utilize it in particular scenarios.

They do this from somebody having this quality, not just as it is one of their actual strengths. For instance, if the circumstance is "setting up an evening gathering for twenty visitors," the therapist requests that the gathering ponder,

1.   What may be the needs or objectives of somebody with your assigned out quality/subject in this situation?

2.   Which questions may somebody with your assigned out quality/subject will, in general, ask in this situation?

3.   What may an individual with this quality/topic do in this situation?

This action emphasizes awareness of personal strengths, strengths in others, and mindfulness. It also shows the estimation of each extraordinary quality inside different situations. This movement is additionally remembered for Activities for Teaching Positive Psychology.

Care Therapy Training and Certification

The Institute for Meditation and Psychotherapy is a non-profit organization. The goal of the establishment is to give training to mental health professionals in the area of coordinating mindfulness meditation and psychotherapy. Their course is for experienced clinicians, paying little heed to the meditation experience.

Members win 72 CE hours through finishing the Certificate in Meditation and Psychotherapy program. It is APA, and NBCC affirmed for the two psychologists and licensed mental health counselors. Nurses and social workers should check the site for more details.

UCSD Center for Mindfulness houses the Mindfulness-Based Professional Training Institute (MBPTI). Through the establishment, you will find certification programs for:

- MBCT,

- MBSR,

- Mindfulness self-empathy,

- Mindful Eating-Conscious Living (ME-CL),

- Mindfulness-based Relapse Prevention (MBRP), Mindfulness-Based Childbirth and Parenting (MBCP), and the sky is the limit from there.

UMASS Center for Mindfulness offers MBSR and MBCT certification online and face to face. You also can take part in MBSR in Mind-Body Medicine, Unwinding Anxiety, or Mindful Eating. This is the place Kabat-Zinn's program started.

All the above projects cost anyplace from a few hundred dollars to a few thousand. The time commitment varies based on courses taken and the area.

Another asset is the International Mindfulness Teachers Association. From their site, you can discover programs for a variety of MBIs.

A Take-Home Message

One of the key takeaways is that research design is critical. The different meta-examinations all incorporate a few requirements for inclusion or exclusion. This, as well, is significant while evaluating their conclusions. Later investigations, however, focus on two fundamental kinds of MBIs (MBSR and MBCT) or derivatives. These, as referenced above, will, in general, give more reliable evidenced-based results.

Some numerous exercises and games reinforce our utilization of mindfulness. Some are bunch situated, while others are explicit to people. You can discover these assets in many forms, including through a helpful relationship, retreats, and telephone applications.

Turning into a prepared care specialist or educator requires extra instruction and can be expensive. Standards for therapists are higher, and licensure is vital in the United States and numerous different countries. By and large, proceeding with education also is a necessity for renewing one's license.

Mindfulness treatment isn't a panacea. It doesn't work for each individual in each condition. However, there is research supporting its use, and current investigations incorporate more rigorous patterns.

Chapter 7 - Getting Resilient Through Cognitive Behavioral Therapy

The mutual foundation of anxiety and depression is an individual's impression of overestimating the risk of a circumstance while thinking little of that they really can adapt. On edge and discouraged, people see numerous risks in a wide range of things: addressing a more interesting, searching for a new position, asking somebody out on the town, etc. In any case, rather than building up the resiliency skills expected to deal with uncomfortable situations, people with anxiety and depression will, in general, keep away from the things they dread or that make them uncomfortable.

Building resiliency is one of the foundations of cognitive-behavioral therapy (CBT). Strength is the capacity to drive forward, to adjust, and to bounce back from difficult situations. Resiliency helps us appreciate life more, adds to our general prosperity, and makes us to acknowledge ourselves as well as other people. Strength empowers us to survive the sadness, disappointments, and pain that is an invariable part of our lives. So, strength greatly contributes to great mental and emotional health and encourages us to endure and adapt and feel in charge in any event, during turbulent times.

Vital to strength are our beliefs. As cognitive-behavioral therapists, we emphasize that because our considerations impact the power of our feelings and our actions, how our opinion about unpleasant or difficult situations also greatly affects our center beliefs. Core beliefs that they are significantly silly or unhelpful, add to anxiety and depression, and also affect our resiliency.

How about we investigate a portion of these unhelpful underlying beliefs:

- I must do everything great, or it's not worth doing by any means.

- It is completely horrible when things are not how I figure they ought to be.

- I ought to be anxious and nervous about anything obscure, unsure, or potentially dangerous.

- I must be loved, liked, or approved of by everybody, constantly.

- It's simpler to stay away from things than to face life's difficulties.

- The world ought to consistently be fair and just.

How a person thinks about difficult situations, his beliefs about his capacities, and his viewpoint toward the future all make an amazing impact on how the individual copes. When an individual is flexible, it's not to state that the individual doesn't have strong feelings—but the resilient person is better ready to direct and control these compelling feelings with the goal that he can react to the circumstance in more proper manners. Emotional regulation has been seen as a significant part of resiliency. Also, resilient people share three sorts of healthy beliefs, which have been described as the "three Cs of resiliency" and have demonstrated to be a defensive factor in anxiety and depression.

The Three Cs of Resiliency

- **Commitment** – accepting that what you do is significant.

- **Control** – trusting you have some impact on the result of occasions.

- **Challenge** – seeing a conceivably upsetting occasion as a test rather than a threat.

Turning out to be resilient is significant. Figuring out how to build the accuracy and flexibility of your reasoning is the first and most significant step in getting resilient to life's unavoidable stresses. Research has discovered that how a person thinks about difficulties and opportunities enormously influences our success in work and school, our risk for anxiety and depression. People who can ricochet once again from difficulty have happier relationships, appreciate better health, and are more effective in their careers and educational pursuits. At Groundwork Counseling in Orlando, our certified cognitive-behavioral therapists (CBT) have particular preparing in strength fabricating. They can assist you in expanding your self-awareness by instructing you to identify your beliefs and find their associations with your feelings and behavior, which is a significant step in increasing resilience.

Assertiveness: What Is Assertiveness?

Have you, at any point, been to a party and found yourself avoiding someone since you didn't have any idea what to state? Have you at any point acknowledged, sometime later, that you had been unfairly criticized or exploited? Is it true that you are hesitant to communicate your thoughts or opinions? Do you discover managing authority figures difficult?

These are instances of circumstances that involve assertive behavior. Assertiveness can be characterized as communication in which one communicates directly and honestly in relational circumstances, while at the same time regarding the rights and dignity of others.

What Is Assertiveness Training?

Assertiveness training can be a viable treatment for specific conditions, for example, depression, social anxiety, and issues coming about because of unexpressed anger. Confidence preparation can also be valuable for individuals who wish to improve their relational abilities and feeling of a sense of self-respect.

Explanations behind Assertiveness Training

Assertiveness training depends on the rule that we as a whole reserve an option to communicate our thoughts, feelings, and needs to other people, as long as we do as such in a respectful way. When we don't feel like we can express ourselves openly, we may get discouraged, on edge, or irate, and our feeling of self-worth may suffer. Our associations with others are also likely to suffer because we may become angry when they don't guess our thoughts for what we are not assertive enough to be letting them know. There are no hard-and-fast rules of what assertive behavior is; somewhat, it is explicit to the specific time and circumstance. Suitably decisive behavior for one individual in one circumstance might be either excessively passive or too aggressive or another person in a different situation. Finally, assertiveness training depends on the possibility that confidence isn't inborn, but is a learned behavior. Although a few people may appear to be more normally confident than others, anybody can figure out how to be more self-assured.

Although these thoughts may sound basic and clear, carrying on, emphatically can once in a while be hard for nearly anybody, and is regularly impossible for some people. Thus, assertiveness training focuses not just on discussing the significance of assertiveness, but also learning assertive behaviors and practicing these practices with the assistance of a professional therapist.

What Is the Difference Between Assertiveness and Aggression?

Individuals, some of the time, confuse assertiveness with aggression, believing that assertiveness preparing may make them pushy or inconsiderate of others. Decisiveness can be thought of as a center point among passivity and aggression. In relational situations, passive behavior occurs when you center on the necessities and wants of someone else; however, overlook your own needs and wishes. In contrast, aggressive behavior happens when you power your own needs on others.

What Is Cognitive Behavior Therapy?

Conduct Therapy and Cognitive Behavior Therapy are kinds of treatments that depend solidly to look into research findings. These approaches help individuals in achieving explicit changes or objectives.

Changes or objectives may include:

- **A method of acting**: like smoking less or being all the more friendly;

- **A method of feeling**: like helping an individual to be less scared, less discouraged, or less anxious;

- **A perspective**: like figuring out how to issue settle or dispose of self-defeating thoughts;

- **A method of managing physical or clinical issues**: reducing back pain or helping an individual adhere to a doctor's suggestions.

Conduct Therapists and Cognitive Behavior Therapists generally center more on the present circumstance and its answer, instead of the past. They focus on a person's views and beliefs about their life, not on character attributes. Conduct Therapists and Cognitive Behavior Therapists treat people, parents, children, couples, and families. Replacing ways of living that don't work well with ways of living that work, and giving individuals more command over their lives, are shared objectives of behavior and cognitive behavior therapy.

The most effective method to GET HELP: If you are searching for help, either for yourself or another person, you might be enticed to call somebody who publicizes in the local distribution or who comes up from a search of the Internet. You may, or may not, find a competent therapist as such. It is wise to mind the qualifications of a psychotherapist. Normally, skillful specialists hold advanced academic degrees. They ought to be recorded as individuals from professional organizations, for example, the Association for Behavioral and Cognitive Therapies or the American Psychological Association. They ought to be authorized to practice in your state. You can discover skillful pros who are partnered with local universities or mental health facilities or recorded on the sites of professional organizations.

The Association for Behavioral and Cognitive Therapies (ABCT) is an interdisciplinary organization committed to the progression of a logical way to deal with the understanding and amelioration of issues of the human condition. These points accomplished through the examination and utilization of behavioral, cognitive, and other proof-based standards to appraisal, prevention, and treatment.

Numerous individuals don't accept that they reserve the option to be emphatic. Many are highly anxious/fearful of being decisive. Many come up short on the social abilities for viable self-expression. Such individuals find situations, like somebody 'cutting in-line' in front of them, managing influential car salesmen, or starting a discussion with aliens to be very difficult and threatening. They appear not to be able to discover the conduct that empowers them to act on his/her health, to take a swing for him/herself without undue anxiety or aggression, to communicate sincere feelings easily, and to practice individual rights without denying the rights of others.

Andrew Salter initially described confidence in the late 1940s as an innate character attribute. Assertive behavior as "communicating individual rights and feelings." They verified that assertiveness was situationally specific: the vast majority can be decisive in certain circumstances, and insufficient in others. Assertiveness training grows the number of circumstances wherein an individual can decide to be confident.

When an individual is passive, opportunities are lost, and unpleasant circumstances are endured. In time, bad feelings can work to a point where one additional occasion can trigger an explosion of resentment that thus incites upsetting analysis or rejection. Stress-related physiological responses can be brought about by extreme passivity or aggression. Behavior that veils undesirable thoughts and feelings may happen, for example, drinking, withdrawal, or obsessing on physical side effects. Non-assertive behavior has been involved in a wide scope of introducing issues, including nervousness, wretchedness, antisocial, aggressive behavior, conjugal disagreement, and low-esteem.

Aggressive communication patterns are not self-assured either. Individuals with a lot of anger, which could be seen as the opposite side of fear, are regularly similarly inadequate in representing themselves. While they may get a quick reaction, their effectiveness in meeting long-range relationship objectives are regularly marred.

Assertiveness training has been utilized with a variety of populations, including grade students, teenagers, students, older, people with a mental health condition (both inpatient and outpatient), professional groups, ladies, heavy drinkers, addicts, and couples.

Most assertiveness training centers on building confident abilities, demonstrating, and practice. The whole chain of practices, verbal and nonverbal, is introduced, and the subject mimics it—the effectiveness of displaying in building up new practices and reducing avoidance behaviors.

While a few clients may do not have an emphatic ability through and through, a practice normally reveals that most clients have a significant number of the necessary parts of expertise, which can be further "shaped" by guidance, positive feedback, and provoking during resulting practice. Practicing new practices in a safe environment reduces discomfort, especially when practice intently takes after the real issue circumstance.

Manifestation Effectiveness

An examination by Lawrence (1970) found significant effects after just 12 minutes of practice. Kazdin (1975) established that covert displaying, in which clients imagine themselves or another person managing social circumstances, was as powerful as real practice.

Graduated schoolwork assignments can allow clients to apply their recently obtained assertive skills first to circumstances in which the probability of success is high, and the level of discomfort is minimal. Initial success will, in general, decrease anxiety, increment the likelihood that clients will sum up the new decisive behavior to different circumstances, and encourage assertive behavior in all the more testing circumstances.

Time for Mastery

The way of turning out to be more assertive is the practice of new behavior patterns. However, there might be some merit to an efficient, step-by-step process that incorporates an understanding of the language and ideas. While the twelve minutes showed above are genuine, and the utilization of Neuro-Linguistic Programming procedures may require close to one-half hour, the comprehensive procedure characterized here, which incorporates showing language, ideas, abilities and giving in vivo practice, is one that is normally spread more than a little while in one-hour segments.

Extraordinary Considerations

A portion of the specific skills of assertiveness may require a development that is past a specific child. The Clinical Supervisor and the Mentor need to decide:

a) If the children are prepared to take the training, as well as

b) How the training is adjusted to enable this particular kid to profit by the experience.

Instructions

The assertiveness training model depicted here emphasizes the structure of assertiveness skills, utilizing model introduction, practice, positive feedback, inciting, covert displaying, and schoolwork assignments. Essential assumptions in regards to one's emphatic rights are made express, traditional assumptions, and fears that inhibit assertive behavior are tested. The advantages and disadvantages of assertive and non-assertive behavior are explored.

"There are three potential wide ways to deal with the lead of interpersonal relations. The first is to consider one's self only and ride roughshod over others, and the second is to consistently put others before one's self. The third approach is simply a brilliant mean. The individual places first, yet considers." - Joseph Wolpe

Step A: Determine Readiness for Assertiveness Training

Discussion: Assertiveness Training can be useful for individuals with either passive or aggressive styles. However, it is regularly better to manage a portion of the issues which provoke these styles before going into Assertiveness Training. This progression is to enable the Clinical Supervisor to make that determination.

Either give the kid Form CBT#23-001 to round out OR peruse and talk about the form with the children. The responses should disclose to you whether the kid is or isn't emphatic in specific areas and help the children perceive where s/he is or isn't assertive.

Assertiveness training is most valuable when the kid can assume the responsibility to recognize social circumstances wherein s/he experiences issues imparting confidently and come up with a lack of certain assertiveness skills, or are not happy in specific circumstances utilizing the self-assuredness skills s/he possesses.

After the summed up form is done, request that the children select a social circumstance wherein s/he didn't share his/her feelings, thoughts, or wishes in a way that allowed him/her to achieve his/her ideal result. Pose a few questions about this circumstance to show signs of improvement in understanding of the issue.

1. "Describe quickly the setting and the individual or people with whom you were communicating."

2. "What did you state and do?"

3. "What was the other individual's reaction to your behavior?"

4. "What did you say to yourself about the situation?" Determine whether the client accepts s/he has an option to be self-assured in this circumstance; regardless of whether s/he anticipates rejection, failure, or some other fiasco if s/he is confident; or if s/he is rewarded here and there for being non-assertive in this circumstance.

5. "What would you have gotten a kick out of the chance to have said or done to achieve a more favorable outcome?"

Determine whether the ideal result can be achieved utilizing assertive behavior.

6. "Have you had the option to do that in any circumstance in the past?" Determine whether before or in different circumstances, the client has had the option to be self-assured in the manner s/he wants, or whether s/he does not have a specific assertiveness skill.

7. "What do you think shields you from doing this?" Determine whether s/he characterizes the obstacle regarding conduct s/he can change, for example, his/her non-assertive behavior, beliefs, or fears. If the kid sees Him/herself as a casualty and sees the main answer for their issues as an adjustment in the earth, the Clinical Supervisor might need to consider an alternate convention to address this issue before doing assertiveness training. This inquiry will also inspire beliefs about the threats of being assertive.

8. "Describe quickly different sorts of social circumstances in which you've experienced issues being decisive and have wound up with not as much as what you truly wanted." Find out with whom they will in general experience issues. If they have a critical indignation issue [controlling their temper], the Clinical Supervisor may conclude that they may profit by a resentment the board preparing before taking an interest in an assertiveness

training. If their idea content is intensely stacked with psychological distortions, the Clinical Supervisor may initially consider subjective rebuilding before attempting assertiveness training.

Clients are suitable for assertiveness training if they demonstrate that they understand that their non-assertive behavior is adding to unwanted results, that they can learn assertive behavior to accomplish their goal, and that it is advantageous for them to meet the necessities of the emphatics preparing to achieve their goals.

Step B. Language and Concepts Conversation Assertive Communication

Assertive communication includes clearly stating your opinion, how you feel and what you need, without damaging the privileges of others. The fundamental supposition in an assertive communication is: "You and I may vary as well as have diverse status [authority/subordinate]. However, we are similarly qualified for communicating deferentially to each other." The significant points of interest of assertive communication remember active cooperation for settling on significant choices, getting what you need without alienating others, the passionate and scholarly fulfillment of respectfully exchanging feelings and thoughts, and high confidence.

Assertive communicators talk in a quiet, intelligible manner of speaking. They look. They have a relaxed, great posture. Exhibit an emphatic trade between an educator and a student:

Teacher: I notice that you haven't completed that paper that should be done on Monday, and here it is Friday. I'm feeling truly tense and in a bad position. I need this done by Monday so I can post the grades. I would especially welcome you going through the end of the week to complete it. If you do, you can have time off next week. If you don't, we will both be in hot water.

Student: Yes, I'm behind on this project. It ended up being more confused than 1 anticipated. I'm not excited about taking a shot at it this end of the week here at school, yet if you let me chip away at it at home on my PC, I guarantee I'll have it done for you for the Monday plan.

Educator: That appears to be sensible to me. Thanks.

Assertiveness is an ability that can be scholarly, not a personality trait that some are brought into the world with, and others are most certainly not. Nobody is consistently assertive. For instance, you may think that it's simple to be assertive with strangers, but experience issues being confident with your folks. You may decide to be self-assured with your friends in a single circumstance and passive or aggressive with them in another. Figuring out how to be assertive means that you can pick when and where to assert yourself.

Aggressive Communication

In aggressive communication, opinions, emotions, and needs may (or may not) be expressed, yet to the detriment of someone else's feelings. Aggressive communicators are normally noisy and direct. They will, in general, have a phenomenal stance and, if possible, tower over others. Mockery, non-serious questions, threats, negative marks, irreverence, you-statements, absolutes, for example, consistently and nobody, finger-pointing, table beating, hands-on-hips, and glaring are a couple of the weapons in their arsenal. Demonstrate an aggressive educator addressing the student.

Educator: You idiot, there are such huge numbers of mistakes in this undertaking I need another eraser! I couldn't care less if you need to remain here throughout the end of the week; get it fixed by Monday or you fail. You're continually missing your deadlines, and you never do things right. You, students, are a lot of worthless kids. This is a direct result of lousy students like you that America is losing its cutting edge on education!

The underlying message is an aggressive communication is: "I'm superior and right, and you're inferior and wrong." The advantage of aggressive behavior is that individuals frequently give aggressors what they need just to dispose of them. The significant disadvantages are that aggressiveness can make others fight back in kind or even in some naughty way. Aggression will, in general, make uncooperative enemies with whom you'll need to deal in the future.

Latent Communication

In passive communication, opinions, feelings, and needs are retained out and out or communicated just partially and indirectly. The passive communicator will, in general, talk delicately. Eye to eye connection is regularly poor, and posture is frequently slouched at this point tense, conveying a message of submission. Demonstrate a passive student reacting to an aggressive teacher.

Student: (softly) I don't need to take this sort of abuse from this jerk!

(So anyone can hear, after a major murmur, with blackout mockery) I'll jump on it immediately.

Step C. Figure out how to Distinguish Between the Three Modes of Communication

Procedure: Give the kid a duplicate of the Six Problematic

Social Scenes. You can put every scene on a three by five card or duplicate it in all. Examine every scene and guarantee that the children understand the concepts of assertive, passive, and aggressive communication and can identify it. You may also choose to make various scenes that are more appropriate to the individual kid you are working with. In any case, if you utilize the joined Form: CBT#23-002, the appropriate responses are as per the following.

Answers:

Scene 1: A forceful. A utilizations sarcasm, rhetorical questions, you-messages, and absolutes. S/he doesn't consider the feelings of B, who turns out to be promptly angry and uncooperative in light of the accusations.

Scene 2: An aggressive. The tone is blaming and accusing. B reacts with hesitance and out of blame.

Scene 3: A is passive. A's shy requests, went before by statements of regret, make it simple for occupied B to state "no."

Scene 4: A is assertive. The request is specific, non-unfriendly, open to the arrangement, and successful.

Scene 5: A is passive. A can't state "no" straightforwardly and rather asks a series of questions, wanting to debilitate B. At last, A comes up with a weak rationalization that B effectively counters.

Scene 6: A is emphatic. She calmly stands up to the prevailing opinion of the gathering and accomplishes a reasonable, non-threatening statement of her position.

Step D. Characterize Criteria for Measuring Change in Assertive Behavior

Procedure: Use the following model and the clear Form: CBT#23-003 for investigating the requirements of the individual kid. Inspect with the kid how the form was rounded out and talk about the ratings of importance and difficulty. After you are certain that the children understand the idea of what is being mentioned, you can give the kid the clear form as homework or fill the form out with him/her.

Step E. Identifying Mistaken Traditional Assumptions and Countering Them with Assertive Rights

Contingent upon the appropriateness, you might need to give the children a copy of Form CBT#23-004, which compares traditional assumptions and individual rights and has a conversation about the conceptual content.

Step F. Going up against Fears about Being Assertive

Conversation: Some children hesitate to carry on decisively because they fear that something bad will happen to them. Three typical fears, fear of failure, and fear of making a dolt of oneself. Here are nine questions and theoretical responses to guide the child in looking at his/her feelings of dread about being emphatic and choosing whether it is justified, despite all the trouble to him/her, to be confident in a specific situation.

Read and talk about the following model with the client. If you are certain that the child understands what is being asked, you can give a clear copy of schoolwork for every particular situation that is being tended to.

CBT#23-0005 SAMPLE Confronting Fears

1.   If I am assertive in this circumstance with someone or others, what is the worst thing that could happen?

(Model: If I ask somebody to the move and s/he says "no," I will feel useless).

2.   What beliefs do I have that would loan probability to this happening?

(Model: I'd need to accept that my value relies on somebody

demonstrating his/her approval of me by accepting my invitation).

3.   Is there any proof to help this belief?

(Model: Not generally).

4.   What proof is there to refute this belief?

(Model: I have esteem that is independent of this current individual's conclusion. I esteem myself as an individual; I have many good characteristics, and I am a good friend, student, musician, and son/daughter).

5.   What would be a more practical negative result of my being assertive in this situation?

(Model: The individual could state "no," in which case I would be disappointed).

6.   How may I react to or adapt to this negative result?

(Model: I would feel disappointed for some time. I would help myself remember my value as an individual and that one rejection doesn't destroy my value. I would converse with my closest friend about it, and then ask another person to the move).

7.   What is the best thing that could occur?

(Model: S/he would acknowledge my greeting, and we would

make some great time).

8.   What will occur if I keep on doing what I have been doing?

(Model: I will spend Friday night at home alone).

9.   Is it justified, despite all the trouble, me to be assertive in this situation? (Weigh your reactions to questions 5-8 preceding answering).

(Model: It merits taking a chance with the mistake of somebody turning down my greeting on the opportunity that I won't need to remain at home Friday night; however, rather will have a date for the move).

Step G. Analysis as a Form of Manipulation

Discussion: The Mentor will talk about with the children the way that numerous individuals experience issues managing analysis since they experience it as a personal rejection. Explore this mentality for this client—How does s/he experience criticism?

Furthermore, for certain clients, all order communication becomes in his/her mind criticism. People who are accustomed to being controlled by others regularly consider all to be as manipulative. For children with issues in living, this experience may also be valid. Request that the child describe times when s/he was criticized? Does s/he incorporate bearing as criticism?

The 'characteristic' reaction is to feel protective when we get an analysis. This is valid for all individuals. The individuals who will, in general, be aggressive in their practices may counterattack; the passive individuals may 'suffer in silence.' Neither one of the responses gives a premise to finding out about yourself nor how others see you. By not defending yourself, you open up the likelihood that you are paying attention to a joke, or accepting a serious comment as an attack. Assertive communication will require attentive tuning in.

So the primary exercise you have to remember is: no focuses on protecting. This means that regardless of what the analysis is, you don't have to protect yourself. If somebody says you're 'insane,' you can ask 'in what manner or capacity?' 'Would it be that I do that causes you to accept that I am 'crazy'?' You may discover that the individual has a point of view that bodes well.

The Mentor should demonstrate this lack of defensiveness all through the engagement. If the Mentor becomes guarded when the children out of anger call him/her a 'jackass' or a 'moron,' it isn't likely that the kid will learn not to be defensive.

Seven [07] assertive strategies for managing analysis will help keep relationships and confidence intact. These methodologies incorporate:

1) Acknowledgment

2) Clouding

3) Testing

4) The content-to-process move

5) Break

6) Easing back down

7) The broken record technique

These methodologies have fundamental ideas that may require that the Mentor tailor them to the one of a kind needs and age development of the children. The Mentor should set aside the effort to talk about these procedures and see how the kid would see utilizing such systems. The Mentor may need to 'role play' every technique to guarantee that the kid 'gets it.' Take as much time on each piece as fundamental. A while later, the Mentor can give 'schoolwork' on every technique or group of systems and have the children record and report on a circumstance where the analysis was given and how the methodology was utilized. Child and Mentor would then evaluate whether the right use happened and the effect that the utilization had on the circumstance.

1. Acknowledgment

When somebody offers constructive criticism, you can utilize this feedback to develop yourself. When you have made a mistake, having somebody call attention to it to you can be useful in preventing future errors.

At whatever point you get criticism with which you agree, regardless of whether it is helpful or a reminder, acknowledge that the critic is correct. Models: 'Truly, I managed to put on one navy and one black sock at the beginning of today. Thanks for pointing it out.' 'You're correct, I am running 30 minutes late with my appointments today.' 'Much obliged for telling me that my voice is too soft for you to hear in the rear of the room.'

You don't have to give excuses or apologize for your behavior. As a child, when asked such questions as 'For what reason did you spill the milk?' or 'For what reason were you ten minutes late?' You may have been required to offer reasonable answers, and, if you didn't have reasonable answers, you might have figured out how to manufacture reasonable excuses. As a developing adult, you can decide to clear your behavior, but you don't have to do as such. Ask whether s/he truly needs to offer a response, or if s/he is simply reacting that exit from habit.

2. Examining

Once in a while, you will be uncertain about the critic's motivation. Is the critic trying to support you and simply going about it awkwardly? Is the critic trying to harm you under the pretense of being useful? Are the pundit's remarks hiding unspoken beliefs, feelings, and desires? Particularly if the critic is somebody who matters to you, you might need to test further into the analysis to respond to these questions. This requires listening carefully—a significant feat when somebody is giving you criticism. Non-constructive, manipulative criticism with which you differ needs some definition. A significant point for the kid to understand is that there is both style and content to criticism. Frequently we get guarded in light of the style of the critic, while the content isn't as dangerous. Listen near the communication and recognize the style and content.

The style might be seen as aggressive and the content valid. Or then again, the style might be seen as only assertive and the content false. Or on the other hand, the content might be seen as both valid and false, relying on specific circumstances. By having no focus on defending and posing the probing questions about the reasons the individual is stating what they are, you may pick up something important to you and others. A great many people who are making an effort not to exploit you will find your non-defensive manner very powerful. The individuals who are attempting to be manipulative will think that it's hard to manage. They need you to be defensive–this is the thing that checks the effectiveness of the attack.

3. Clouding

When you have determined that the analysis is more to glorify the critic than to serve you, this may deserve the assertive method known as clouding. Clouding is an attempt to 'cloud' the critic's issues by proceeding with a non-defensive reaction, through a procedure of defusing the content. The manipulative critic, for the most part, takes a grain of reality and expounds on it, utilizing his/her sufficient creative mind to put you down. For example: 'Williams, late with that report? You're in every case late. I can't imagine how you have gotten this far with your inadequate work habits. Why, if everyone in this school were as slow and lazy as you are, we would need to hang a lounger in every classroom!'

What would it be a good idea for you to tune in for? Manipulative critics are master at verbally abusing and you-messages. They raise the old history. They use absolutes, for example, consistently, never, and everybody, so these are keywords to tune in for. If you are foolish enough to try to prevail upon them, you just give them more ammunition for their case. They are not keen on tuning in to you, in any event, when they ask you a question. Their delicate personalities expect them to be correct and to win their point consistently.

When you're enticed to justify yourself or fight back in kind to manipulative analysis, advise yourself that you will just take care of a senseless argument which you can't in any way, shape, or possibly win. If you are as yet unconvinced, reflect occasions you have attempted to reason or settle the score with a manipulative critic. Why keep on burning through your time doing something so horrendous and useless? As another option, figure out how to stop manipulative critics in their tracks.

Then again, it is hard for us all too simply sit and tune in to a manipulative critic and not have some 'nasty' thoughts, which fuel some compelling feelings that make it difficult for us to not react with a behavior that is probably going to raise the issue. While this is valid for every manipulative critic, it is particularly hard for a children, whose critic is an individual of power. That is the reason it is essential to show effective ways to diffuse manipulative analysis through agreement.

a. Agree in Part

The principal way includes discovering some piece of the manipulative critic's statement that you believe is valid and concurring with it. Rethink the critic's sentence with the goal that you can genuinely agree. Drop the absolutes. Ignore the remainder of the message. In light of the model simply expressed, you may essentially answer, 'You're correct, I am late with this report.'

The critic will, for the most part, try to drive you into conceding further bad behavior. However, if you keep on discovering some piece of what the critic is starting to concur with, s/he will before long feel worn out on trying to prove that s/he is correct and you are incorrect. It isn't a very remarkable test to argue with somebody who continues to agree with you.

b. Agree in Probability

The second type of clouding you can use with a manipulative critic requires that you discover something in what the manipulative critic is stating with which you can likely concur. You can internally contemplate that the chances of his/her being correct are one out of many as you answer: 'You're presumably right that I'm regularly late.' Again, change the wording marginally, so you don't compromise your honesty and agree with something you don't accept.

c. Concur in Principle

The third and last type of clouding includes agreeing with the manipulative critic on a basic level. This requires simple logic: if X, at that point, Y. 'If everybody in the school were as slow and lazy as you state I am, we would need to reduce the desire and have a special school.'

4. Content-to-Process Shift

When your discussion with somebody gets obstructed due to strong feelings or as a result of a conflict of requirements or needs, move the focal point of the discussion from the subject to an examination of what is happening among you.

For instance, you are assertively asking your friend to talk with you more, and s/he reacts with: 'You feel like I'm ignoring you? Why I remember a period, you hardly spoke to me.' Rather than getting into a fruitless argument about the past, you answer: 'You seem, by all accounts, to be angry with me.' You express a basic perception of the idea of the connection while ignoring the substance of the association.

The motivation behind this instrument is to recover the discussion moved to the first subject and away from the manipulative analysis. Common issues that you may have in practicing content-to-process move just because of include:

- Lapsing into a clarification of why the other individual has gotten out of control when the reason for this tool is essential to bring up that the discussion has been crashed with the goal that it very well may be welcomed on target once more.

- Being blamed for psychoanalyzing the other party as a ploy to limit the content-to-process move. A good reaction to this is, 'I'm essentially expressing my supposition, and then to come back to the first theme.

- Being told that the procedure remark isn't right. As opposed to getting into a discussion, use acknowledgment or clouding, and then come back to the first point.

- Rigidly sticking to the first theme when the content-to-process move remark has raised something that would best be settled before your arrival to the first subject. This is especially obvious when the other party has a plan that is so important to him/her that it prevents him/her from perceiving yours.

5. Break

When you arrive at a stalemate in a discussion, you might need to defer the discussion until some other time. The break is helpful when the collaboration is either too passive or too aggressive. You might be quiet, crying, occupied, unready to make a decision, or agreeing with everything different says. Or on the other hand, maybe you is hitting below the belt by name-calling, raising ancient complaints, or being manipulatively critical. If you or the other individual feels also pressured to communicate or think right now, allow yourself to chill, ponder what has been stated, and return later with the positive aim of communicating rather than only demonstrating your point and winning. For instance, in light of an individual who is pouting, you confidently get a break: 'This is certainly not a good time to resolve our difference of opinion. We should discuss it tomorrow.'

6. Easing back down

Try not to imagine that you need to respond immediately to every situation. You don't need to create a moment answer. Numerous individuals accept that they don't think well 'on their feet' and need to mull things over before a reaction. When the other individual doesn't imagine that way, the discussion may wind up going too quickly, with one creation a reaction that they may not like after they consider it. Momentary delays allow you to:

1.   Be sure that you understand what the speaker has said.

2.   Process what has been said.

3.   Become mindful of what you think, feel, and need concerning what has been said.

4.   Avoid making statements that you may regret later.

5.   Consciously impact the circumstance toward the result you need.

Common statements that you can use to hinder a connection include:

- This is too critical to even consider racing through, we should back off.

- That's an interesting point, let me consider it for a second.

- Wait a moment. I need to offer you my honest answer.

- Is this what I hear you saving? (Repeat what you think you heard while setting aside an effort to take it in and ponder it).

- I'm not certain I understand, would you be able to state that once more?

7. Broken Record Procedure

The broken record procedure is one of seven assertive skills that will enable the children to bargain all the more viably with uncooperative and manipulative people.

The way into the messed up record strategy is persistent repetition in the face of adversity. The child should be helped to remember his/her legitimate rights, so s/he isn't controlled into yielding to people whose interests are strife with his/her own. Sometimes, you experience individuals–sales reps, children, or a stubborn friend–who won't take 'no' for an answer. When you have a legitimate position as far as possible, and another person is experiencing issues getting your message, you have to stand firm and stick to it. This isn't a technique to avoid following the directives of a parent or potentially educator, basically because you 'don't feel like it.'

This methodology is additionally compelling in mentioning to individuals what you need when their desires are keeping them from seeing yours.

1.   Decide what you need or don't need. Review your thoughts about the circumstance, your emotions, and your rights.

2.   Create a brief, exact, easy-to-understand statement about what you need. One sentence is ideal. Give no reasons or explanations. Try not to state, "I can't." The other individual will call attention to you; this is simply one more reason and gives you how you can. It's a lot less difficult and more honest to state,

"I would prefer not to." Eliminate any escape clauses in your brief statement, which the other individual could use to advance their position.

3.   Use non-verbal communication to help your statement—great stance, direct eye to eye connection, and a quiet, confident, and determined voice.

4.   Firmly repeat your short explanation the same number of times as fundamental for the individual to get your message and to understand that you won't adjust your perspective. S/he will most likely concoct various reasons or essentially state "no." In the long run, even the most forceful individual will come up short on no's and excuses, if you are persistent. Change your short articulation just if the other individual finds a serious loophole in it.

5.   You might need to recognize the other person's opinions, feelings, or needs before coming back to your broken record. But, don't feel committed to addressing questions. Be mindful so as not to be diverted from your goal.

Chapter 8 - Self-Esteem

What are simply the basic highlights of Low Esteem?

When our impression of ourselves is negative, it can prompt a mind-boggling sentiment of low self-esteem; "I'm sufficiently bad,"; "not fascinating enough," as well as "I am not appealing enough."

These are not simply transient negative automatic thoughts that we, as a whole, would have time to time in a specific troublesome circumstance. However, in low self-esteem, these are worldwide thoughts regarding the self that continue reoccurring.

When an individual with low self-esteem enters troublesome circumstances, a negative belief about oneself is initiated. This produces negative expectations, about what could turn out badly, and creates nervousness and a low state of mind. To redress or stop the awful expectation, from happening, we can avoid potential risk. These activities, expected to adapt, can strengthen the negative belief or "contaminates" the result, and thus affirming the core belief.

For instance, we can quit seeing our friends, going out to do the food shopping from fear of being reprimanded or decided by others – so we can get disengaged. Also, when we do see others, we may feel it is essential to help other people and please others, however much as could reasonably be expected, if not "I will be dismissed, relinquished, disliked." and so on.

Can CBT Therapy be utilized for Low Self Esteem?

In low self-esteem, cognitive behavioral therapy (CBT) believes that these core beliefs are simply suppositions, not realities, which are kept up by unhelpful thinking or practices. To beat low self-esteem, we utilize a standard arrangement of techniques demonstrated to try out these beliefs and build up another arrangement of supportive practices. The point is to check whether these beliefs rise to prove and if not to distinguish elective 'rational' understanding about how things are.

Cognitive-behavioral therapy (CBT) centers on our thinking errors and retrains the mind to think in an increasingly adjusted manner, and it centers on practices to make them progressively functional.

If we have the idea that an individual has quite recently disregarded me and that implies I am sufficiently bad, maybe a progressively adjusted idea may be that the individual was distracted and may have a couple of issues to manage. Rather, subsequently, of returning home and sitting idle and accepting this idea as 'truth,' maybe a 'call to this individual to check whether they are okay, maybe an increasingly accommodating behavior; helping us to affirm/disapprove the underlying idea we may have had comparable to this circumstance.

Treatment typically incorporates:

- Cognitive rebuilding

- Analysis of at present held Schema

- Behavioral Activation

- Behavioral Experiments

- Social Skills training

- Decisiveness Training

- Roleplay

- Mindfulness training

Low self-esteem implies not having a favorable opinion of yourself as an individual, or not holding yourself in high respect. If you have low confidence, you probably won't feel sure or competent, feel anxious, and criticize yourself harshly. Psychologists think that underneath sentiments of low confidence are the negative beliefs and suppositions we hold about ourselves. A few people realize that their negative judgment of themselves is excessively cruel; others clutch these convictions so certain that they can feel like realities. Luckily, there are useful psychological approaches for improving your confidence.

How is it to have low self-esteem?

Daniel's belief that he was useless and extraordinary

Daniel was the most youthful of four kids. Growing up, he adored comic books and film, and he proceeded to consider filmmaking at school. Scholastically he wasn't as brilliant as his sisters, something he felt his folks reprimanded him for. Daniel had a little gathering of companions; however, he was tormented at school. He came to accept that he was inept, 'extraordinary,' and useless. He would get bothered when encircled by individuals he thought of as increasingly skilled, never felt agreeable around women, and never felt like he fit in. Daniel turned out to be extremely self-critical. He believed he must be watching out for his defects to attempt to conceal them from others before they took note.

Parts of treatment that Daniel found helpful

Daniel thought that it was useful to think about his negative beliefs as a feeling instead of a reality and to comprehend where this opinion had originated from. The part of treatment that he discovered most accommodating was the point at which his advisor acquainted him with testing his self-critical voice. It felt irregular in any case, yet rapidly, he started to see that his sense of worthlessness had no premise. He had left school and had begun college which allowed him the chance to try different things with demonstrating sides of his character that he hadn't felt okay with previously: meeting individuals with comparable interests helped him to grasp his 'distinction' as a positive characteristic lastly begin to feel good in his skin.

What Causes Low Self-esteem?

CBT is always keen on what props an issue up. This is supposing that we can work out what props an issue up. We can get the issue by interceding intrude on this maintenance cycle. Two treatment programs for low self-esteem have increased specific noticeable performance.

A psychologist called Melanie Fennell built up an influential cognitive-behavioral model of low self-esteem. Fennell's model says that you structure negative beliefs about yourself for an amazing duration, which she called your 'bottom line.' Your bottom line is frequently an (excessively basic) depiction of yourself and may be summed up as something like "I'm useless" or "I'm nothing but bad." Your bottom line is consistently there, lazy, yet gets initiated specifically circumstances. When it is enacted, you are bound to utilize some safety strategies:

- **Addressing yourself in a basic manner**. Regularly expected as an approach to persuade yourself, all the more frequently this winds up hindering you, and it strengthens your bottom line.

- **They are setting resolute rules about how you ought to be**. We set ourselves 'rules for living,' which are planned to shield us from having our most noticeably worst fears confirmed. The issue is that they are not truly adaptable, and can defy the guidelines that can prompt increasing self-criticism.

- **You are making anxious predictions about what may occur**. If we don't consider ourselves to be skillful and fit, the world frequently feels brimming with risk. Your anxious mind attempts to help by predicting potential threats; however, this fair causes us to feel considerably increasingly unfit.

- **Evasion and wellbeing strategies**. If you figure your imperfections may be uncovered, it bodes well to attempt to avoid that threat. Be that as it may, you don't get an opportunity to figure out how well you could have adapted.

Fennell says that although these wellbeing methodologies can cause you to feel great for the time being, every one of them implies that your bottom line never shows signs of change, and your self-esteem doesn't improve.

What props is low self-esteem going?

A therapist called Kees Korrelboom built up another model of low self-esteem, which depends on present-day thoughts of how memory functions. Korrelboom's thought is that occasions throughout your life lead you to frame a negative self-image—a kind of picture in your mind of what your identity is. When you experience a prompt (for instance, somebody says, "who are you?"), your mind consequently recovers this mind could retrieve it. Korrelboom says that there are quite of adaptations of 'you'—and loads of 'pictures' that your mind could recover—yet it gets into the habits for recovering an extremely negative one, and the outcome is low self-esteem. Korrelboom's model says that the reason self-esteem endures is a result of the 'habit' that your mind has of recovering the exceptionally negative image.

Treatments for low self-esteem

Psychological treatments for low self-esteem

Various psychological treatment has been created, which directly target low self-esteem: these incorporate cognitive-behavioral therapy (CBT), and competitive memory retraining (COMET). There is evidence that both are compelling types of treatment.

Medical treatments for low self-esteem

There are no suggested medical treatments for low self-esteem without anyone else. Low self-esteem goes with different scatters; for example, tension or depression, medical treatment might be suggested.

How might I overcome my low self-esteem?

There are loads of things that you can accomplish for yourself that will assist you in overcoming low self-esteem. The tasks and self-esteem worksheets depicted beneath are adjusted from both the Fennell and Korrelboom approaches. Although they depend on marginally different theoretical backgrounds, there is no motivation to feel that they are inconsistent. These include:

- Testing your anxious predictions, moving toward circumstances that you have been abstaining from, lessening your security practices (behavioral experiments)

- Distinguishing and testing your self-criticism (thought records)

- Retraining yourself to concentrate on the positive

- Changing your rules and assumptions

- Testing your bottom line and building another one

- Practicing positive parts of your self-image with the goal that they 'win' the memory retrieval competition

Testing your anxious prediction

Anxious minds are centered on danger: their main motivation is to guard us. Restless personalities make expectations about negative things that may occur, yet they regularly take a 'best to be as cautious as possible' approach. The outcome is an inclination of anxiety. When we are feeling anxious, we will, in general, get things done trying to have a sense of security –, for example, avoid from circumstances or avoiding potential risk if we do need to go up against them. One issue of avoiding from or utilizing 'security practices' is that we never get the opportunity to see if our restless expectations are valid. A few things that you can do are to monitor your anxious predictions utilizing thought records, test how precise your anxious expectations are by utilizing behavioral expectations, or use decatastrophizing procedures to calm your anxious mind.

Distinguishing and challenging your self-criticism

We as a whole address ourselves, and when we do it in empowering ways, we can feel great. However, individuals with low self-esteem frequently have an unforgiving and critical inner voice. A few therapists like to consider this a 'bully voice.' The psychologist Paul Gilbert regularly utilizes a relationship about the kind of teacher you would need for a child: OK need one who is brutal and correctional or one who is caring and strong? One method of conquering low self-esteem is to change how we address ourselves or to have an alternate relationship with your inner voice. A portion of the techniques that psychologists instruct incorporate checking your self-critical contemplations utilizing self-esteem worksheets like the self-basic idea observing record, testing your negative thinking utilizing thought records, and finding out about your unhelpful thinking styles.

Retraining yourself to concentrate on the positive

The psychologist Christine Padesky contrasted our most difficult convictions with blind individuals. She said that they rush to spot anything terrible related to the thing they are biased against, yet practically oblivious in regards to great affiliations. She gives a case of 'Sigmund' who has an extreme that women are inferior compared to men:

Therapist: "Okay, presently, when Sigmund sees a woman, and she isn't working out quite as well as a man at a task, what does he say?"

Client: "Sigmund calls attention to how ladies are consistently inadequate."

Therapist: "Presently, what does Sigmund say when a woman is accomplishing something too or far superior to men—has this at any point happened when you were around Sigmund?"

Client: "Ordinarily, he just disregards it and discover something to condemn—their appearance, or their attitude."

The purpose of this is our negative beliefs make us focus on one-sided ways. If your main concern is "I'm a disappointment," you are *much* bound to focus on your battles than your triumphs. The issue of this 'biased perception' is that you just observe a large portion of the image–you don't get the chance to see yourself decently, and nothing changes. One accommodating strategy is to utilize a self-esteem worksheet like the positive conviction log: your test recognizes a portion of your positive characteristics and gives close consideration to times in your day that delineate these.

Testing your bottom line and building another one

Eventually, you should comprehend what your primary concern is. On the off chance that you have checked your self-basic musings you may have seen themes in the sorts of considerations you have, or the sorts of marks you apply to yourself. CBT specialists regularly utilize the descending bolt method as a method of investigating individuals' main concerns. It may be useful to treat your main concern like an assessment or a hypothesis to be tried. Numerous individuals think that it's supportive of concocting some primary elective concerns (regardless of whether they don't generally trust them with everything that is in them yet) and afterward to gather proof in their day by day life to see which conviction (old main concern or new positive conviction) is a progressively precise perspective on the world. This frequently takes determination, yet it pays off.

Changing your rules and presumptions

Fennell's model says that our low self-esteem beliefs can be 'secured' (kept up) by our implicit principles and suppositions. For instance, Rai had consistently thought of herself as 'stupid' and held the presumption if anybody censured her; it implied that she had committed an error and was dumb. Where it counts, Catherine thought she was unlovable and clutched an inclination that she would possibly be acknowledged whether she was the correct size and shape. The issue of rules is that they are frequently unnecessary, absurd, and excessively severe: they're not genuine guidelines about how the world functions. However, are presumptions that keep us stuck in unhelpful ways and behaving. The adjusting rules and presumptions worksheet is an organized method of inspecting how your rules operate.

Practicing positive parts of your self-image with the goal that they win the memory retrieval competition

Korrelboom's model of low self-esteem depends on a thought regarding how your memory functions. When you are given a signal, say somebody says "speedy, think about an animal" your memory can choose from any of the animals that you think about, say giraffe, rhino, elephant. But, it needs to pick one, and it will pick the one that rings a bell most promptly: maybe you thought of a dog or a feline since they're your top choice because you live with one. Memory works like this for mental self-portrait as well. Suppose the signal is "brisk, consider what sort of individual you are" – your memory could choose from many, state graciousness, persistence, mindful, thoughtful. However, for individuals with low self-esteem, it might be in the 'habit' or picking from all around practiced negative characteristics, which you probably won't care for about yourself. This thought regarding how memory functions are called retrieval competition and Korrelboom built up treatment for low self-esteem dependent on this standard called Competitive Memory Retraining (COMET). Contrasted with Fennell's CBT approach, the COMET approach works more with mental images. A portion of the means of the COMET protocol include:

- Recognizing your negative self-image

- Naming the opposite self-portrait (gather characteristics that contradict your negative self-image)

- Recognizing instances of your opposite self-portrait

- Use imagination exercises to work on making the opposite self-image especially important

Chapter 9 - Sleep disorders

A sleeping disorder is a common sleep disorder that can make it difficult to nod off, difficult to stay asleep, or cause you to get up too soon, and not have the option to return to sleep. Cognitive-behavioral therapy for a sleeping disorder, some of the time called CBT-I, is an effective treatment for chronic sleep problems and is generally suggested as the first line of treatment.

Cognitive-behavioral therapy for insomnia is an organized program that encourages you to distinguish and replace thoughts and practices that cause or compound rest issues with propensities that promote sound sleep. In contrast to sleeping pills, CBT-I encourages you to defeat the fundamental reasons for your sleep problems.

To recognize how to treat your insomnia best, your sleep therapist may have you save a definite rest journal for one to about fourteen days.

How does cognitive behavioral therapy for sleeping disorders work?

The cognitive part of CBT-I instructs you to perceive and change beliefs that influence your ability to sleep. This sort of therapy can assist you in controlling or taking out negative thoughts and stresses that keep you conscious.

The behavioral part of CBT-I causes you to develop good sleep habits and avoid practices that shield you from sleeping well.

Depending upon your requirements, your sleep therapist may suggest a portion of these CBT-I techniques:

Stimulus control therapy. This method helps evacuate factors that condition your brain to resist sleep. For instance, you may be instructed to set steady sleep time and wake time and keep away from snoozes, utilize the bed just for sleep and sex, and leave the room if you can't rest inside 20 minutes, possibly returning when you're tired.

Sleep restriction. Lying in bed when you're wakeful can turn into a habit that prompts poor rest. This treatment diminishes the time you spend in bed, causing incomplete lack of sleep, which makes you increasingly worn out the following night. When your sleep has improved, your time in bed is step by step expanded.

Sleep hygiene. This method of therapy includes changing basic lifestyle habits that impact rest, for example, smoking or drinking an excessive amount of caffeine late in the day, drinking an excess of alcohol, or not getting normal exercise. It additionally incorporates tips that help you sleep better, for example, approaches to unwind an hour or two preceding sleep time.

Sleep environment improvement. This offers ways that you can make an agreeable sleep environment, for example, keeping your room tranquil, dull and cool, not having a TV in the room, and concealing the clock from view.

Relaxation training. This method encourages you to quiet your mind and body. Approaches incorporate contemplation, symbolism, muscle relaxation, and others.

I am remaining passively awake. Called paradoxical intention, this includes staying away from any push to nod off. Incomprehensibly, stressing that you can't sleep can keep you alert. Relinquishing this concern can assist you in unwinding and make it simpler to fall asleep.

Biofeedback. This method permits you to observe biological signs, for example, heart rate and muscle pressure and tells you the best way to alter them. Your sleep specialist may have you take a biofeedback device home to record your everyday designs. This information can help recognize designs that influence sleep.

The best treatment approach may consolidate a few of these methods.

Cognitive-behavioral therapy vs. pills

Sleep medications can be an effective short term treatment—for instance, and they can give prompt help during a time of high pressure or sadness. Some more current sleeping medications have been endorsed for longer use. However, they may not be the best long term insomnia treatment.

Cognitive-behavioral therapy for a sleeping disorder might be a good treatment choice if you have long term rest issues, you're stressed over getting reliant on sleep medications, or if drugs aren't powerful or cause bothersome side effects.

In contrast to pills, CBT-I tends to the fundamental reason for insomnia instead of simply diminishing indications. Yet, it requires significant investment—and exertion—to make it work. Sometimes, a combination of sleep medication and CBT-I might be the best approach.

Insomnia and other disorders

Insomnia is connected to various physical and mental health disorders. Progressing absence of sleep expands your risk of wellbeing conditions, for example, hypertension, coronary illness, diabetes, and chronic pain. A few meds, including over-the-counter prescriptions, additionally can add to insomnia.

If you have a condition or prescription that is connected to a sleeping disorder, converse with your PCP about how best to deal with these alongside rest issues. A sleeping disorder is probably not going to show signs of improvement without treatment.

Finding help

There is a predetermined number of confirmed Behavioral Sleep Medicine specialists, and you may not live almost a specialist. You may need to do some looking to locate a trained practitioner and a treatment timetable and type that fit your needs. Here are a few spots to look:

- The American Academy of Sleep Medicine site permits you to look for an affirmed sleep community, for example, Mayo Clinic Center for Sleep Medicine.

- The Society of Behavioral Sleep Medicine site offers an index for finding a behavioral sleep medicine provider.

The kind of treatment and recurrence of sessions can fluctuate. You may require as not many as two sessions or upwards of at least eight meetings, contingent upon your sleep master, the program, and your advancement.

When calling to set up an arrangement, get some information

about their methodology and what's in store. Additionally, check early whether your health insurance will cover the kind of treatment you need.

If accessible in your area, meet with a sleep medicine specialist face to face for your meetings. In any case, telephone conferences, CDs, books, or sites on CBT techniques and a sleeping disorder additionally might be helpful.

Who can benefit from cognitive behavioral therapy for sleep deprivation?

Cognitive-behavioral therapy for insomnia can profit almost anybody with sleep problems. CBT-I can help individuals who have essential sleep deprivation just as individuals with physical issues, for example, ceaseless torment, or mental health disorder, for example, depression and tension. Furthermore, the impacts appear to last. Furthermore, there is no proof that CBT-I has negative symptoms.

CBT-I requires consistent practice, and a few approaches may make you lose sleep from the start. In any case, stay with it, and you'll likely observe lasting outcomes.

Therapy for Sleep Disorders

When you're frantic for sleep, it tends to be enticing to go after a sleeping pill or an over-the-counter tranquilizer. In any case, sleep medication won't fix the issue or address the hidden indications—indeed, it can frequently exacerbate sleep issues in the long term. Saying this doesn't imply that there will never be a period or a spot for sleep medicine. To avoid reliance and resistance, however, sleeping pills are best when utilized sparingly for medical procedures, for example, bridging time regions or recouping from a medical procedure. Regardless of whether your sleep disorder requires the utilization of prescription medication, experts suggest joining a medication routine with treatment and sound way of life changes.

Cognitive-behavioral therapy can improve your sleep by changing your behavior before sleep time, just as changing the perspectives that shield you from falling asleep. It centers on improving relaxation skills and changing ways of life propensities that sway your sleeping patterns. Sincerest issues can be both brought about by and trigger passionate medical issues, for example, anxiety, stress, and depression, treatment is a successful method of rewarding the hidden issue instead of simply the manifestations, helping you create healthy sleeping patterns forever.

An ongoing report at Harvard Medical School found that CBT was more powerful at treating chronic insomnia than remedy sleep medicine. CBT created the best changes in patients' capacity to fall asleep and stay unconscious, and the advantages stayed even a year after treatment finished. In case you're experiencing a sleep disorder, treatment might have the option to loosen up your mind, change your standpoint, improve your daytime propensities, and set you up for a good night's rest.

What characterizes a sleep disorder?

Sleep disorder is a condition that, as often as possible, effects your capacity to get enough quality rest, leaving you feeling depleted or sleepy during the day. The most well-known sleep issue incorporates a sleeping disorder, sleep apnea, narcolepsy, restless legs syndrome (RLS), and circadian rhythm sleep disorder frequently activated by move work or jet lag.

Cognitive-behavioral therapy (CBT) for sleep disorders

Cognitive-behavioral therapy is the most broadly utilized treatment for sleep disorders. It might be led exclusively, in a group of individuals with comparable sleeping issues, or even online. Since the causes and side effects of sleep issue change impressively, CBT ought to consistently be custom fitted to your particular issues. Psychological conduct treatment for a sleeping disorder (CBT-I), for instance, is a particular kind of treatment intended for individuals who can't get the measure of sleep they have to wake up feeling refreshed and revived.

The length of the therapy additionally relies upon the sort and seriousness of your sleep issue. While CBT is once in a while a quick or easy cure, it is a relatively short term. Numerous CBT treatment programs for a sleeping disorder, for instance, report significant improvement in sleep patterns following a course of 5 to 8 weeks after weekly sessions.

How accomplishes CBT work for sleep disorders?

CBT addresses negative patterns and behavior that add to a sleeping problem or other sleeping issues. As the name recommends, cognitive behavioral therapy includes two primary segments:

Cognitive therapy instructs you to perceive and change negative beliefs and considerations (discernments) that add to your sleep issues.

Cognitive therapy shows you how to stay away from practices that keep you alert around evening time and supplant them with better sleep habits.

Utilizing a sleep diary in CBT

To distinguish patterns in your sleeping issues and choose the best treatment approach, your therapist may begin by requesting that you keep a sleep diary. The subtleties can be significant, uncovering how certain practices are destroying your opportunity for a good night's sleep.

Thought to challenge in CBT

The cognitive parts of CBT incorporate thought challenging—also called cognitive restructuring—in which you challenge the negative thinking patterns that add to your sleep issues, supplanting them with progressively positive, practical thoughts. The thought is that if you change how you want to, change how you feel, and at last, how you sleep.

This includes three steps:

1. Distinguishing your negative thoughts. If you have a sleep issue, for example, a sleeping disorder, you may see the impediments that keep you from getting a good night's sleep to be more noteworthy than they truly are. For instance, you may continue disclosing to yourself that you can't nod off except if you take a sleeping pill. The more you disclose to yourself that, the more restless you'll become if you don't take a pill and the harder you'll see it to sleep.

2. Testing your negative thoughts. In the subsequent step, your therapist will show you how to assess your sleep-disrupting thoughts. This includes scrutinizing the evidence for your considerations, breaking down unhelpful beliefs, and testing out the truth of negative predictions.

3. Supplanting negative thoughts with reasonable thoughts. When you've distinguished the negative mutilations in your thoughts, you can supplant them with new contemplations that are increasingly precise and positive. Your therapist may assist you in thinking of sensible, calming statements you can say to yourself as you're planning for sleep.

Testing negative thoughts that fuel sleep issues

Unrealistic expectations

Negative thoughts: I ought to have the option to sleep soundly consistently like an ordinary individual.

Sleep promoting comeback: Lots of individuals battle with sleep every once in a while. I will have the option to lay down with practice.

Exaggeration

Negative thought: It's the equivalent every night, one more night of restless hopelessness.

Sleep promoting comeback: Not consistently is the equivalent. A few evenings, I show improvement over others.

Catastrophizing

Negative idea: If I don't get some sleep, I'll tank at work and imperil my activity.

Sleep promoting comeback: I can get past work regardless of whether I'm worn out. I can at present rest and loosen up today around evening time, regardless of whether I can't rest.

Hopelessness

Negative thought: I'm never going to have the option to sleep well. It's out of my control.

Sleep promoting comeback: Sleep issues can be relieved. If I quit stressing such a lot and spotlight on positive arrangements, I can beat it.

Fortune telling

Negative thought: It's going to take me, in any event, an hour to get the chance to sleep in his evening. I simply know it.

Sleep promoting comeback: I don't have a clue what will happen today around evening time. Possibly, I'll get the chance to rest rapidly if I utilize the new procedures I've learned.

Since negative thoughts are frequently part of a long-lasting pattern of thinking, supplanting negative thoughts with increasingly sensible ones is seldom simple. Be that as it may, with training, you can break the habit. That is the reason it's essential to practice the techniques you learn in treatment, all alone at home.

Behavioral techniques utilized in CBT for sleep disorders

Just as changing how you consider sleep, CBT additionally attempts to change the habits and practices that can keep you from sleeping well. Depending upon your particular indications and necessities, your advisor may utilize a portion of the accompanying techniques:

Sleep restriction therapy (SRT) lessens the time you spend lying in bed conscious by eliminating naps and constraining you to keep awake past your ordinary sleep time. This method for lack of sleep can be particularly powerful for a sleeping disorder. It does not just make you progressively worn out the following night yet constructs a more grounded relationship among bed and sleep than bed and lying awake.

Sleep control therapy assists in distinguishing and change sleep habits that keep you from sleeping well. This implies preparing you to utilize your room for simply sleep and sex, as opposed to working or sitting in front of the TV and keeping up predictable sleep-wake times, even on ends of the week.

Improving your sleep condition and sleep hygiene. Your sleep environment ought to be dull, calm, cool, and agreeable, so your therapist may suggest blackout shades, earplugs, or a sound machine to shut out the noise. Sleep hygiene includes improving your daytime propensities to incorporate practicing normally, avoid from nicotine and caffeine late in the day, and figuring out how to loosen up around evening time.

Remaining passively awake, otherwise called "paradoxical intention." Since agonizing over not having the option to rest creates uneasiness that keeps you awake, relinquishing this concern and putting forth no attempt to sleep may incomprehensibly, help you to loosen up and fall asleep.

Relaxation training. When rehearsed normally, relaxation techniques, for example, care reflection, dynamic muscle relaxation, and breathing activities can assist you in relaxing around evening time, easing strain and nervousness, and setting you up for sleep.

Biofeedback utilizes sensors that measure explicit physiological functions, for example, heart rate, breathing, and muscle strain. Biofeedback instructs you to perceive and control your body's tension reaction that effects sleep patterns.

Hypnosis can now and then be utilized in CBT for the sleep disorder. While you're in a condition of deep relaxation, the hypnotherapists utilize diverse therapeutic techniques to assist you in changing negative thought patterns or unhelpful propensities and promote restful sleep.

Relaxation techniques for insomnia

Abdominal breathing. Breathing profoundly and completely, including the chest, also the tummy, lower back, and ribcage can enable you to unwind. Close your eyes and take profound, slow breaths, making every breath significantly more profound than the last. Take in through your nose and out through your mouth.

Progressive muscle relaxation. Make yourself agreeable. Beginning with your feet, tense the muscles as firmly as could be expected under the circumstances. Hold for a check of 10, and afterward relax. Keep on doing this for each muscle bunch in your body, stirring your way up to the highest point of your head.

Mindfulness meditation. Sit unobtrusively and center on your regular breathing and how your body feels at the time. Permit thoughts and feelings to travel every which way without judgment, continually coming back to concentrate on your breathing and your body.

Making therapy work for you

Making enhancements to your sleep regularly requires some serious time and commitment. It's basic that you therapist a therapist who's directly for you: somebody who you can trust, somebody you feel good conversing with, and somebody who will fill in as an accomplice in your recuperation. When you've discovered the correct therapist, it's critical to stay with treatment and follow your therapist's recommendation. In case you're feeling debilitated with the pace of recuperation, recall that treatment for sleep issues is extremely successful over the long haul. You'll receive the rewards if you oversee it.

You can bolster your treatment by settling on a positive way of life decisions that advantage your ability to sleep.

Add increasingly physical activity to your day. Exercise relieves stress and tension and improves sleep, so set aside a few minutes for regular exercise. Focus on 30 minutes or more on most days—yet not very near sleep time.

Be smart about what you eat and drink—and when. Keep away from delayed dinners inside two hours of sleep time. Quit drinking stimulated refreshments at least eight hours before bed. Like caffeine, nicotine, and sugary foods are energizers, and keeping in mind that alcohol can make you sluggish, it meddles with the nature of your sleep and can exacerbate sleep disorder symptoms worse.

Diminish pressure and anxiety in your life. If the stress of work, family, or school is keeping you conscious, you may require help with stress management. By dealing with worry profitably, and keeping up a quiet, uplifting standpoint, you'll have the option to sleep better at night.

Chapter 10 - Cognitive Behavioral Therapy for Addiction

Cognitive Behavioral Therapy, or CBT for short, is a sort of "talk" therapy, given the mental principles of behaviorism—which is about how individuals' practices can be controlled or altered, and theories of cognition—which are centered around seeing how individuals think, feel, and get themselves and their general surroundings.

Behaviorism centers on the practices or moves an individual makes, while speculations of comprehension center around individuals' discernments—what they see, hear, and feel their thoughts, and their feelings. CBT is a variety of behavioral therapy that centers on changing behavior through matching positive and negative reinforcement, rewards and disciplines, and practices that the individual needs to increase or decrease.

The human experience of discernment incorporates our recognitions, contemplations, feelings, and comprehension. This incorporates everything that comes into our mind through our faculties, or through how we think our past encounters—adding analysis of cognition to behavior therapy by the advancement of cognitive-behavioral therapy by considering individuals' considerations and sentiments about their practices. Rather than simply watching and controlling practices, there is additional consideration paid to what is happening in the mind of the individual and how those discernments, contemplations, and feelings lead them to carry on specific ways.

CBT especially investigates the contentions between what we need to do and what we do. Addiction is a good example of this sort of conflicted behavior- we may comprehend what is healthy and safe, which is to stay away from addictive practices and substances. Yet, we decide to feel free to take part in the behavior at any rate, in some cases prompting extremely upsetting ramifications for ourselves and others. And individuals with addictions may lament these practices, it may be difficult to quit rehashing them, some of the time without the individual truly knowing why.

Cognitive Behavioral Therapy for Addiction

Addiction is a clear example of an example of behavior that conflicts with what the individual encounters it needs to do. While individuals attempting to defeat addictive practices will frequently say they need to change those practices and may need to stop liquor, drugs, or other impulsive practices that are messing them up, they discover it incredibly hard to do as such. As indicated by the cognitive behavioral therapy approach, addictive practices, for example, drinking, drug use, issue betting, urgent shopping, computer game compulsion, food addiction, and different kinds of unsafe, unnecessary behavior, are the consequence of off base contemplations and resulting negative feelings.

Cognitive-behavioral therapy clarifies this by explaining the way that individuals' thoughts and feelings collaborate. Therapists understood that a considerable lot of us have contemplations, in light of beliefs that are false, unreasonable, or difficult to satisfy, and these musings, like this, cause negative emotions that feed tension, melancholy, and conditions like enslavement. By methodically recording our considerations and related sentiments, alongside the occasions that trigger those thoughts and emotions, and the conduct that we do this, we can start to change the programmed forms that harm our endeavors at changing our behaviors.

By looking at patterns of contemplations and emotions that we experience, we can start changing those thoughts by deliberately looking at circumstances in more practical ways that don't consequently prompt negative feelings and patterns of harmful behaviors. By compensating ourselves for the more advantageous practices, we supplant those harmful behaviors. After some time, the more advantageous practices become related to progressively positive feelings and become increasingly automatic.

CBT has an excellent track record, with various examinations showing its adequacy in treating depression, tension, and different conditions, including habit.

The CBT approaches that became advanced towards the finish of the twentieth century are themselves being refined and supplanted by the alleged "third wave" of behavior therapy, which centers on mindfulness, acknowledgment, and being at the time. These approaches incorporate Acceptance and Commitment Therapy (ACT), Dialectical Behavioral Therapy (DBT), Mindfulness-Based Cognitive Therapy, and Functional Analytic Psychotherapy.

Cognitive-behavioral therapy enables an individual to expel self-disrupting thoughts, which fuel medication or alcohol misuse. All the more explicitly, it centers on how an individual's considerations impact their sentiments and practices. By seeing how these components are associated, an individual is better prepared to think and act in a positive way that supports collectedness.

What an individual thinks, how they feel, and how they act massively affects their life and wellbeing, particularly during recovery. When these elements are grounded in constructive propensities, they increment an individual's prosperity and sober living abilities. Then again, ought to these be useless, an individual could encounter damage to their life, well-being, and recuperation.

As a feature of addiction treatment, cognitive behavioral therapy enables an individual to stand up to and adapt to thought patterns and issues throughout their life which drive addictive behaviors.

What Is Cognitive Behavioral Therapy?

Cognitive behavior therapy is a combination of two therapeutic approaches, psychological treatment, and social treatment. As psychotherapy, or "talk therapy," the dependent individual and therapist assemble a therapeutic alliance that utilizations talking as a way to promote healing and the learning of healthy behaviors. Instances of psychotherapists who offer these types of assistance incorporate therapists, psychologists, licensed professional counselors, and licensed social workers.

Rather than analysis, which centers intensely on the past, cognitive behavior therapy is a problem-oriented strategy that enables an individual to look at broken patterns inside their present life. Past events aren't disregarded. However, the attention is on helping an individual distinguish and change current thoughts, emotional reactions, and practices that are harming their life and recuperation.

Role of Cognitive Behavioral Therapy in Addiction Treatment

A mind changed by addiction can make an undesirable environment of negative considerations, variable feelings, and impulses for drug use. Together, these components can color how an individual identifies with their encounters and change how they see their substance abuse. Combined with any prior patterns of antagonism or psychological instability, this imbalance can fuel drug abuse and lead an individual to self-medicate.

It may be hard to deal with the problematic contemplations and feelings life brings when calm. For an addicted person, this can be devastating without assistance and direction from an expert.

Negative thoughts and the harmful practices resulting from them can go about as a trigger for medication or alcohol abuse. Breaking this cycle through treatment enables an individual to prevail inside the treatment and manufacture a solid foundation for recuperation.

While certain outpatient projects may offer cognitive behavioral therapy, this treatment might be better utilized in a residential inpatient drug rehab program because of the serious idea of the sessions.

Which Types Of Drug Addiction Does Cognitive Behavioral Therapy Treat?

While cognitive-behavioral therapy might be utilized to get to treat various medications of abuse, investigate shows that it's progressively viable for specific types of substance maltreatment than others. As indicated by the National Institute on Drug Abuse, cognitive behavioral therapy is an evidence-based way to deal with chronic drug use treatment for:

- Alcohol

- Marijuana

- Cocaine

- Methamphetamine

The researchers found that the best treatment results were related to marijuana. From that point forward, cocaine and opioids saw the best outcomes. In any case, the littlest impacts were seen in people who had poly-substance or polydrug dependence. This implies people who are struggling with addiction on more than one substance may profit all the more completely from another type of treatment or a combination of medicines.

Cognitive behavior therapy has been appeared to deliver enduring outcomes when used to treat different kinds of addiction. For example, the article referred to one investigation that "revealed that 60% of patients in the CBT condition gave clean toxicology screens at 52-week follow-up."

Benefits of Cognitive Behavioral Therapy

Each individual living under the weight of addiction has exceptional conditions that brought them there—recognizing and rewarding individual issues that prompt drug or alcohol abuse assists in decreasing triggers and self-destructive practices.

Cognitive behavior therapy has been appeared to:

- Help an individual recuperate from injury.

- Construct coping skills that diminish the effect of stress.

- Help an individual handle feelings more healthily.

- Help individuals resolve issues in their relationships.

- Reinforce an individual's communication skills.

- Help an individual adapt to sadness or misfortune.

- Help an individual arrangement with chronic medical illness.

- Diminish or mitigate certain side effects of mental

sicknesses.

- Prevent a backslide of these side effects.

- Fill in as a treatment for a mental illness when drugs can't be utilized.

Left unaddressed, a large number of these issues may make individuals use medications or alcohol as a method for keeping away from the pain or distress brought about by these circumstances.

Length of Cognitive Behavioral Therapy Treatment

Probably the best advantage of cognitive behavioral therapy is its escalated approach and moderately short treatment time when contrasted with different therapies. Regularly, an individual may have a week after weekly sessions for five to 20 weeks, totaling 10 to 20 sessions. The specific length of treatment and frequency of sessions may differ contingent upon a person's particular needs and treatment goals.

There are a few components that impact an individual's treatment plan. These incorporate the:

- Explicit conditions or disorder(s).

- Level of indications an individual encounters.

- Period an individual has been struggling.

- Level of pressure an individual is confronting.

- Level of help an individual has from loved ones.

The psychotherapist giving these medicines can enable an individual to decide the correct treatment plan for their necessities. As treatment advances, this arrangement might be changed to all the more likely to oblige an individual's recuperation objectives and current life conditions.

What's to expect At Cognitive Behavioral Therapy Sessions?

During a CBT session, the therapist will manage an individual towards recognizing and beating ruinous and negative thoughts, which could subvert their quest for temperance. Cognitive-behavioral therapy can occur in an individual, gathering, or family setting, which can all be useful during addiction treatment.

In the first session, the therapist will clarify the therapeutic procedure, answer any questions, and assess the issues an individual needs to take a shot at. In the sessions that follow, the therapist will enable the individual to take a shot at unmistakably characterized issues and objectives which center on them. To help these goals, an individual may have "homework." This may incorporate working on adapting methodologies and monitoring any problematic thought patterns which emerge.

Altogether, for the therapist to perceive what an individual needs to chip away at, the person in treatment needs to open up about their struggles. This incorporates discussing the considerations and sentiments which revolve around them.

While it very well may be at first difficult for an individual to open up and feel helpless, the more genuine an individual is with themselves and their therapist, the more noteworthy their ability for progress.

To empower this receptiveness and promote healing, CBT has a few objectives, including:

- Recognizing the issues or conditions which are associated with addiction.

- We are building up the consciousness of negative contemplations, emotions, and practices which add to the addiction.

- I recognize negative perspectives or deceptions that addictive behaviors worse.

- They were assessing why these considerations happen

and how they can be reshaped or dispensed with positively.

During therapy, an individual will get familiar with an assortment of fundamental abilities and recovery techniques that can help them upkeep their sobriety, for example,

- Decisiveness

- Adapting skills

- Relaxing aptitudes

- Versatility

- Stress management skills

There are no known significant reactions or threats from subjective social treatment, in any case, it is normal for an individual to feel some proportion of uneasiness or distress when they initially recognize troublesome issues or feelings they're attempting to survive. As treatment proceeds, these emotions should diminish and make an individual more grounded and ready to effectively carry on with a medication-free life.

Cognitive Behavioral Therapy in Use with Other Therapies

Cognitive behavior therapy has indicated incredible achievement in rewarding habits when utilized alone or as a major aspect of a treatment plan that uses different therapies. However, most normally, in recovery programs, CBT will be bolstered by an assortment of different treatments tailored to an individual's special needs. During addiction treatment, these treatments may incorporate alternative therapies, other research-based behavioral therapies, and additional prescriptions (pharmacotherapies).

Progressing research proposes that cognitive-behavioral therapy may, by and large, be increasingly compelling when utilized with different treatments, most eminently contingency management (CM) (or similar methods), and motivational interviewing(MI).

Also, dialectical behavioral therapy, a specific type of CBT, is an evidence-based psychotherapy that utilizes traditional components of CBT in an organization with others focused on ways to deal with treat addiction. Dialectical behavior therapy shows care, acknowledgment, and pain resilience, all abilities which can be inconceivably advantageous during recovery.

Commonly, a combined approach better helps an individual evacuate unsafe impacts, practices, and thought designs that energize addictive behavior and go about as triggers for relapse. Utilizing various therapeutic techniques enables an individual to create adapting and relapse prevention skills custom fitted to the existing conditions they'll likely face after treatment.

Whenever therapy is utilized, the specific structure and combination of medicines ought to be guided by an individual's individualized treatment plan. By and large, the behavioral therapies utilized during fixation treatment are impacted by different worries in an individual's life, for example, a dual diagnosis.

Role of Cognitive Behavioral Therapy in Dual Diagnosis Treatment

Notwithstanding substance abuse, cognitive behavioral therapy is an examination based treatment for various mental and physical medical issues, a significant number of which much of the time happen with addiction.

Similarly, as negative contemplations feed addictive practices, they decline the indications of certain mental illnesses. If these psychological instabilities aren't tended to and rewarded, they can compound the habit or trigger a relapse? When an individual has both a psychological wellness and substance use issue, it's named a co-happening issue or dual diagnosis.

Psychological instability and addiction are regularly firmly associated. As a rule, one causes or exasperates the other. If one disorder is dealt with, the other can go about as a trigger. For example, if an individual drinks alcohol to numb the feeling of discouragement brought about my misery, the untreated depression could make them break sobriety and drink once more.

Cognitive-behavioral therapy can enable an individual to sustain their mental and emotional wellbeing. By figuring out how to think in a progressively positive way, an individual is increasingly adept at having adjusted feelings and settle on more beneficial decisions. Thus, these changes support and proceed with restraint. Much more, CBT has been appeared to alter brain activity, persuading that it improves by and large brain working.

Instances of mental health disorders which have indicated achievement when rewarded with CBT:

- Anxiety disorder

- Bipolar disorder

- Depression

- Eating disorder (for example anorexia, bulimia, and binge-eating disorder)

- Obsessive-compulsive disorders

- Fears

- Post-traumatic stress disorder (PTSD)

- Schizophrenia

- Sexual disorder

- Sleep disorder

Further, CBT has been appeared to lessen symptoms identifying with chronic pain. This can be especially useful for individuals who initially started drug abuse as an approach to self-treat torment. Opioid painkiller abuse as often as possible starts in this way.

For these people, elective types of pain management are significant pieces of building restraint and a strong recovery. By assuaging some proportion of these side effects, the trigger (pain) is diminished, diminishing the allurement for self-medicine and drug abuse.

Keeping up restraint is a difficult journey, and keeping in mind that drawn-out progress can be based on treatments, for example, this, positive results are upgraded by a solid support network, including alumni aftercare services.

Chapter 11 - Achieve work-life balance

Work-life balance. Maybe an expression that is abused to such an extent that it has become, to some degree, empty or even mythical. When we think about work-life balance, we, as a rule, envision an adjusted state wherein our time is carefully isolated among work and other life exercises, for example, time with family, exercise, and entertainment. When I have conversed with individuals about their thoughts on work-life balance, generally, the accord is many people might want to achieve; however, feel like they are never effective in accomplishing. This made me imagine that possibly, work-life balance isn't something that can be "attained." Further, when we consider it that way, it turns into a win big or nothing phenomenal: it is possible that you have it or you don't. The issue with that perspective on work-life balance is that in actual existence full of unpredictable events, it is practically difficult to be in finished parity regular. Feeling like we "fizzled" at it could prompt defenselessness and surrendering.

A progressively supportive and practical way to deal with work-life balance is to consider it a goal, or something that we can generally be moving in the direction of, regardless of whether we are not in every case effectively living in a perfectly balanced state. From this point of view, the goal is to do as well as can be expected to locate a solid equalization for ourselves on some random day, and this may fluctuate from every day. For instance, on days where work requires a ton of our consideration, equalization may be simply discovering the opportunity to eat and rest. On different days, a balance may be going home ahead of schedule to fit in practice and go to the recreation center with your children. Trying toward work-life balance ordinary takes into consideration greater adaptability and more chances to settle on choices that will push you toward work-life balance, regardless of whether you are not generally in perfect balance.

Trying toward work-life balance can affect well-being, feelings of anxiety, relationships, and state of mind. Here are a few hints to assist you in discovering more parity consistently.

1) Keep track of what you do consistently for a multi-week. Toward the week's end, assess how you invested your energy and contrast it with how you might preferably want to invest your time. Pick one thing in the week that you could do any other way to push you closer toward your ideal balance.

2) Use your values as a manual for making more balance in your life. Make a list of qualities or a rundown that is generally essential to you in your life and what you need your life to represent. Values could incorporate family, companions, hardworking attitude, offering back to the community, otherworldliness, and so on. It is hard to live following the entirety of your qualities ordinary since we may have values that are contending. For instance, it might be hard to keep in contact with companions when you have a bustling work routine. When esteems are contending, organize. Regardless of whether it is ordinary, week, or month, consider what is generally imperative to you and do things that are following that. When your needs to change (for instance, a friend in need may take need overwork), change how you separate your time. This could help add to a healthy balance.

3) Plan ahead. Without purposely planning activities that could add to more adjust, we may consistently discover a reason to linger. As such, it is critical to plan for exercises that add to adjust, a similar way that you would plan a gathering at work. If you keep a schedule, take a stab at including "go to the gym" (if that is a part of your healthy lifestyle) in your schedule instead of simply perceiving how you feel toward the day's end. Scheduling it improves the probability of finishing.

4) Think a little. On those days that your balance will be not exactly perfect, don't simply surrender! Keep in mind, and work-life balance doesn't need to be a win or bust marvel. Consider little ways you can progress in the direction of somewhat more parity on a busy day. For instance, go for a brief stroll outside, send a quick text to a companion, or eat a healthy snack.

5) Respect how you decide to invest your energy. For instance, when you choose to set work aside, truly do it. It is enticing to browse that last email, yet will it truly have any kind of effect? No doubt, it won't have any kind of effect in your work; however, it will have any kind of effect by the way you feel.

How to Have a Healthy Work/Life Balance

Current life forces more worry than any other time in recent memory, as we get ourselves unfit to actualize limits between our work and home lives. It is essential to build up a sound work-life balance with the end goal for us to lead balanced and satisfying lives.

We figure it would be simple not to work, yet psychological studies and specialists feature that we have to work to genuinely and intellectually bolster our home life, as well. In this post, Blue House Yoga is going to look at which strategies ought to be considered for discovering balance as estimated by the Hierarchy of Needs. Generic self-care exercises, for example, spoiling, digital detoxes, and practice, are prescribed over the web to bring balance into your life. Look at strategies and procedures that will execute long haul improvement to your work-life balance and genuine positive change as opposed to conventional solutions.

CBT and Yoga

Yoga is an antiquated and all around perceived strategy for dealing with life's day by day pushes. Proceeded with training develops mindfulness and welcomes care which will help sort out an amazing needs.

However, to adequately handle the origin of your stress and to execute long term improvement in both your work environment and home life, consider CBT. CBT is an educational and explorative approach that draws in with and intensifies the principles of yoga; emotional well-being, cognitive thoughts, and physical sensation.

Blue House Yoga teacher Daniela De Silva is a thorough well-being guide. Daniela is qualified with unique excellence in CBT (Cognitive Behavioral Therapy) and can assist you in discovering equalization and agreement in your life. This all-encompassing way to deal with treatment is proven and can be joined with a yoga system that improves CBT. The collaborative combination mix of methods empowers the person to target both the indications of tension just as the main drivers of the stress.

CBT is the best technique for overseeing nervousness while yoga revives the person. This implies you will have the apparatuses to decrease the effect of working environment worries just as the impression of more opportunity to handle present wild-day lives with a progressively uplifting disposition. Using this procedure, your satisfaction will be immeasurably improved.

Well-being in the Workplace

Guaranteeing you have a healthy work/life balance is the duty of the person as much as the business. Employers who promote mental and passionate agreement and adaptability in the working environment help their group's inspiration, profitability, and maintenance. Studies have demonstrated that businesses that offer adaptable working profit by a 75% reduction in enlistment expenses and sickness absence rates fall by 25%. It was accounted for this week that a New Zealand organization that have trialed a four-day work-week has seen "no drawback," and each part of the business has improved.

This is an aftereffect of people having the option to deal with their own time and consolidate self-care to support psychological well-being and revive the body and brain. Remember that work is similarly as significant as life; it introduces reason and gives a feeling of significance and having a place. Frequently, it can be utilized to structure our lives (even with adaptable working hours) and gives strength, which is required for accomplishing self-actualization of one's maximum capacity on Maslow's Hierarchy of Needs.

If it is beyond the realm of imagination to expect to have adaptable hours in your work environment, consider requesting team building activities that will support social fulfillment just as the sentiment of having a place with a group. Studies show that organizations that give group building exercises have an 85% improvement in inside correspondence, expanded innovativeness, and worker fulfillment. This is because the exercises welcome the social commitment and lessen worry from the working environment. Then again, put aside an ideal opportunity to get familiar with another expertise or something in your standard that is intellectually satisfying. This will animate your cognitive, esteem, and maybe stylish requirements, contingent upon your picked side interest. Yoga and CBT can show you how to see this as an approach to mitigate pressure as opposed to another thing on your daily schedule.

To bring corporate yoga into your work environment, or to discover increasingly about how our complete well-being and yoga teacher can assist you in actualizing a more beneficial, agreeable way of life, connect with us today.

How we deal with our functioning day is changing as new technologies permit us to be always adaptable. While once, not very far in the past, we were stuck at our work areas in a single office encompassed by a similar gathering of individuals, we may now be telecommuting or hot-desking either inside a single structure or from numerous areas.

With this new working arrangement, laborers can feel strain to be accessible 24 hours every day, and some may contact focused if they are not close by when their supervisor calls.

Simultaneously, individuals may want to stay in contact with companions using social media while at work, so it doesn't merely work affecting home life. Yet, home life coming into the workplace as well–a 'work/life combine.'

It is regularly felt that mobile technology permits work to hinder home life, and many have ascribed rising degrees of worry to this circumstance. Anyway, ongoing research completed by First Psychology's Professor Ewan Gillon and Dr. Lisa Harrow, found that while this might be the situation for certain individuals, others feel more pressure when they can't stay in contact with work.

So stress is a personal thing, and what stresses one individual eases stress in another. It is significant for individuals to be in charge of how they utilize mobile technology so they can utilize them to best profit their work and their style of working. Essentially forcing one method of working for everybody is counter-profitable and can make pointless worry among employees.

Tips to get technology working in support of yourself

If you like to keep in touch with work while away and discover this decreases your feelings of anxiety:

- Allot times during the day for checking messages and put forth a conscious effort not to check outside of these times.

- Make some set memories each night when you switch off your cell phone to permit yourself to be technology-free before bed.

- Put forth an attempt to concentrate on your loved ones when you are with them and taken care of the versatile. A quick check of messages between courses or when you utilize the loo will keep you feeling in control.

If you feel invaded by technology:

- Utilize technology in patterns where you need it to work flexibly, for example, if you are off work hanging tight in for a plumber or you are away on business.

- Put aside times to browse and answer to messages during the day so you can continue ahead with what you're managing without constant interruption.

What was evident from our examination was that mobile

technology could be both companion AND foe; it's how you use it that issues, and for it to turn into a companion, the choice on how it's utilized must be close to personal to you.

Chapter 12 - Guilt

Guilt is a feeling people normally have in the wake of accomplishing something incorrectly, purposefully or inadvertently. An individual's feeling of guilt usually identifies with their ethical code.

Guilt isn't terrible. Some of the time, it's even gainful. Feeling bad after committing an error can prompt change, for example, an apology or a decision to settle on various decisions later on. A "guilty pressure" can portray something innocuous an individual appreciates regardless of whether they believe they shouldn't or are humiliated about their tastes.

In any case, the blame is now and then unhelpful. It can cause physical side effects, self-doubt, diminished confidence, and disgrace. It tends to be hard to defeat these sentiments, particularly on account of constant blame. Yet, it is conceivable, particularly with help.

If you are struggling with feelings of guilt, contact a certified guide who can assist you in getting to the foundation of these emotions, comprehend why they endure, and assist you in tending to them. Doing so can help keep them from influencing you contrarily.

What Is Guilt?

It isn't easy to understand what guilt is. Indeed, guilt and shame are frequently mistaken for one another. However, they're particular feelings. Guilt depicts a feeling of disappointment or obligation that identifies with activities taken. Individuals may feel they coerce over things they fouled up, things they accept were their flaw or things they had no obligation regarding. Survivor's guilt, for instance, can influence individuals who endure disasters when numerous others passed on.

Individuals watch out just to feel guilt over activities they see as "bad" or "wrong." An individual who accepts they are qualified for a higher compensation may take modest quantities of cash from their manager while never feeling guilty. But, an individual who finds a wallet and keeps the cash inside without putting forth any attempt to see the money may feel as liable for a considerable length of time or even years, if they accept the "right" activity would have been to turn in the wallet.

A few people experience chronic guilt, which can prompt sentiments of insufficiency. This type of guilt can prompt destructive activities rather than positive change. Individuals may control others with what's known as a "guilt trip" by utilizing an individual's blameworthy emotions as an instrument to them to do what they need.

Somebody who feels guilty about something they did might find a way to address their mix-up, apologize, or in any case, offer some kind of reparation. This generally makes sentiments of guilt abatement.

In any case, shame, which depicts a lament or awareness of other's expectations that identifies with oneself, can be progressively hard to address. It's not simple to diminish sentiments of shame, particularly shame that isn't completely comprehended. Individuals, once in a while, feel embarrassed about some piece of themselves without knowing why. An individual may feel shame when others think about activities they feel regretful over.

Shame can make individuals feel dishonorable or, in one way or another, insufficient. It might prompt detachment, demonstrations of self-discipline, or other possibly unsafe practices.

Guilt Psychology

Guilt is a molded feeling. Individuals are molded (they figure out how) to feel regretful. Certain elements may make it almost certain individual encounters incessant or over the excessive guilt. These components may incorporate their way of life, family, or strict childhood. If parents reliably cause a kid to feel blameworthy or reliably retain acclaim, for instance, the kid may come to feel that nothing they do is ever sufficient. This can prompt a guilt complex.

Individuals who struggle to beat sentiments of interminable blame may have a higher hazard for wretchedness, uneasiness, or other emotional well-being concerns. Individuals who have emotional wellness issues may, like this, become overpowered by blameworthy sentiments about their psychological state or related practices. An individual with gloom who self-secludes may feel remorseful for closing out their companions but cannot help but do as such.

Guilt that identifies with past slip-ups or disappointments can set an individual up for proceeded with struggles. Some of the time, guilt can shield an individual from having satisfying associations with others.

Kinds of Guilt

Research associating guilt and psychology doesn't generally concur. A few investigations have discovered that guilt may help shield individuals from emotional distress. Others propose guilt, particularly over the top guilt, which adds to emotional and mental pain.

When all is said and done, there are three different types of guilt.

Reactive guilt: Reactive guilt happens when an individual accepts that they have acted against their personal belief of what is ethically acceptable or the guidelines society has for adequate behavior.

Anticipatory guilt: This guilt is the aftereffect of contemplating acting against good individual guidelines or the measures of society. An individual may decide not to make a specific move since they realize it isn't right or trusts it might hurt others.

Existential guilt: This guilt can be progressively confused. Existential guilt can depict an individual's affections for general foul play or the possibility that "Life isn't reasonable." It can portray the guilt an individual feels for the negative effect they may have on the lives of others.

A few scientists further divide guilt for two classes. These classifications can be considered independently from the above types of guilt.

Maladaptive guilt: This sort of guilt regularly negatively affects life. This guilt may incorporate constant blame (coerce that identifies with shame) and other guilt that prompts mental or emotional distress.

Adaptive and pro-social guilt: This sort of guilt is accepted to be useful, as it identifies with an individual's comprehension of bad behavior and obligation.

Various sources can add to the guilt

Family

A kid, by and large, finds out about "right" and "wrong" from relatives, particularly guardians. When a child gets out of hand, guardians will typically communicate dissatisfaction and issue a result. Realizing their parent is baffled may trigger sentiments of disappointment. The child might need to do whatever they can to win back endorsement from their parents.

Culture

When an individual's way of life holds that specific conduct isn't right, an individual may feel remorseful regardless of whether their own ethical code lets them know there is nothing wrong with the behavior. An unmarried individual raised in a culture that demoralizes sexual connections outside of marriage may feel remorseful when they have intercourse, regardless of whether they trust it's totally fine to engage in sexual relations without being married.

A guilt culture stresses the impacts of an individual's conduct on others and interfaces this to how that individual is seen by others. When an individual's activities cause others damage or misery, that individual loses cultural regard, or "face." Until they present appropriate reparations, they are frequently observed as "disfavored" according to society. In blame societies, fixing the error, saying 'sorry'/as well as by one way or another creation revises can fix the damage.

Religious Beliefs

Some strict conventions underscore they coerce more than others. If an individual's activities aren't following the lessons of the religion, coerce frequently originates from their belief that a heavenly force knows their activities and considers them responsible. This regularly drives an individual to admit their wrongs, atone (an activity inside oneself), and plan something to fix an inappropriate.

The possibility of a "guilty conscience," or an inner voice that tells somebody when they've fouled up, isn't carefully strict, yet it is frequently part of strict conventions. An individual who feels regretful might be asked by this inner voice to fix their misstep in one way or another.

Society

Guilt can come about because of stressing what others will think about specific convictions or conduct. Society can highly affect an individual's feelings of guilt. Realizing that others may see and judge activities can influence an individual's decisions. This blame can be something to be thankful for, as it bolsters the accepted practices or good standards individuals by and large following, for example, "It's inappropriate to take" or "If I hit somebody's left vehicle, I should leave a note with my telephone number and name."

Impacts of Guilt

The mental impacts of guilt can be valuable when they move an individual to make changes in their conduct. However, on different occasions, they can cause trouble. Research has indicated that guilt and despondency are regularly connected, for instance. Research additionally recommends that anxiety, just as over the obsessive-compulsive disorder (OCD), can be identified with sentiments of guilt or shame.

When an individual can't fix a mistake, guilt can persevere until they get the opportunity to present appropriate reparations. Guilt coming about because of an activity that can't be fixed, for example, when an individual feels they in a roundabout way caused another's demise, can have an enduring, negative effect on life. Treatment can regularly enable an individual to address these feelings and reframe their sentiments about what occurred.

Another impact of guilt is a guilt complex. This is diligent guilt over mischief an individual accepts they have caused. They might not have done anything incorrectly, yet they live in dread, but they will accept that they are continually committing errors and "can't do anything right." A guilt complex can be related to anxiety and shame. It might identify with an individual's youth: When guardians are excessively objecting or retain acclaim, children may much of the time feel regretful for what they see as their "badness."

Physical Symptoms of Guilt

Individuals with uncertain guilt may feel touchy or consistently nervous. They might be excessively tenacious or contrite.

Sentiments of guilt additionally frequently show as physical indications. These might include:

- A sleeping disorder or trouble sleeping

- An annoyed stomach, sickness, or other digestive issues

- Stomach pain

- Muscle strain

- Head pain

- Tearfulness

By and large, tending to the guilt will help settle these side effects.

Conclusion

The journey of CBT is about to end in this book. We learned that CBT might be adequately adjusted for use with older adults by applying minor changes to clinical techniques since the principles of the psychological and behavioral theory are thought to be comparable for older and younger adults. Choosing which alterations to make, and how to lead them, depends on a total comprehension of the different changes inborn in the aging process because of improvement, accomplice contrasts, and the social setting of older adults. Applying CBT to more former clients involves a few difficulties, including finding out about the social condition of older adults, working with clients whose encounters might be not quite the same as and before those of the therapist, and managing the exchange of physical and mental issues frequently. The individuals who take on the challenge will probably find that their thoughts regarding therapy and aging will be changed by working with older clients.